FAST & FRESH BABY FOOD COOKBOOK

FAST & FRESH
Baby Food

120
Ridiculously Simple and Naturally Wholesome
Baby Food Recipes

JACQUELINE BURT COTE

in collaboration with

**ROCKRIDGE
PRESS**

Contents

CHAPTER SIX 12 TO 18 MONTHS

Real Meals and Snacks

Getting a Healthy Start

• • • • • • • • • • • • • • • • • • • •

Welcome to the wonderful world of making solid food for your baby! Whether you're planning ahead or eager to start making purées tomorrow, get ready for countless messy, surprising, rewarding, frustrating, and hilarious experiences. Eating and sleeping are two of parents' greatest preoccupations during the first year of their baby's life. While your child's sleep is largely out of your control, what you feed your baby is entirely—and usually literally—in your hands.

All parents want to give their babies the healthiest possible start, and there's no better way to do that than by feeding them the most nutritious and delicious foods on the planet. But while natural homemade fare may be the most wholesome option for little ones (and big ones, too), not all parents feel they have the time or energy to prepare baby food from scratch. That's why so many busy moms and dads find themselves resorting to prepackaged purées: They're fast, easy, and virtually mess-free.

Making your child's meals in your very own kitchen is actually much easier and less time-consuming than you might think. Whether you're just introducing your baby to solids or teaching your toddler the joys of feeding himself, this book will help you prepare simple but flavorful everyday meals that can be prepared and cooked in 30 minutes or less, and are a snap to store.

At this point in your little one's life, all that's necessary are different combinations of fresh and flavorful whole foods.

As you read, you'll also learn about basic cooking methods, necessary tools and equipment, the importance of opting for organic groceries (and what to choose when you can't), which foods are highest in antioxidants (and why antioxidants are so valuable to your baby's diet), how to avoid allergic reactions, and much more.

Conveniently organized by age, each recipe chapter starts with clear-cut advice on your child's development, his nutritional needs, and which foods he may be ready to try, as well as tips on dealing with individual taste preferences and phases—like what to do

when your toddler is more interested in throwing dinner on the floor than putting it in his mouth.

Best of all, this book is packed with recipes for every stage of your baby's growth, from four to eighteen months. If the recipes sound simple, it's because they are. Slaving away in the kitchen does not equal good parenting. At this point in your little one's life, all that's necessary are different combinations of fresh, whole foods, which pack both flavor and the complete nutritional punch that nature intended. Feel free to make the recipes as you see them, or let the different food pairings inspire you to experiment.

Beginning with cereals and one-ingredient purées and moving on to combination mashes and toddler meals such as Apple Pie Oatmeal Purée (page 55) and Butternut Squash "Mac and Cheese" (page 121), these dishes are so delectable that you just might find yourself finishing your little one's leftovers—if he doesn't gobble everything up first, that is!

CHAPTER ONE

Only the Freshest Ingredients

· ·

As a new parent, your top priority is making sure your baby has everything she needs to be happy, healthy, and safe. In these first months of your child's life, a well-balanced diet of fresh, nourishing food serves as the foundation for many years to come, providing the building blocks for both short-term and long-term development. By preparing your baby's food at home, you can help ensure your little one gets everything she needs and nothing she doesn't—namely, added hydrogenated fats, sugar, and oils, as well as potentially harmful chemicals in the form of flavorings, dyes, pesticides, and preservatives.

Plus, you'll find that homemade meals simply taste better than their store-bought counterparts. This is because most commercial baby foods are heated to extremely high temperatures in order to extend their shelf life, a process that unfortunately diminishes flavor, texture, and even some vital nutrients along with bacteria. Relying on prepackaged foods can also deprive your baby of much-needed variety, because highly perishable ingredients (avocado, melon, and many leafy greens, for example) are rarely found in the nonrefrigerated sections of the supermarket.

Finally, preparing your child's food at home can turn out to be far less expensive in the long run than buying endless jars at the store, potentially saving you hundreds of dollars per year.

OPTING FOR ORGANIC

If you're not familiar with what makes a food "organic" and why organic foods are often preferable to nonorganic—particularly for kids—here's what you need to know.

Organic fruits, vegetables, dairy, and meat are produced without the addition of synthetic chemicals such as fertilizers, pesticides, herbicides, fungicides, antibiotics, or hormones such as bovine growth hormone, also known as rBGH. It's worth noting that rBGH has been banned in Europe and Canada; major U.S. companies such as Starbucks, Yoplait, and Dannon have also gone rBGH-free.

According to the U.S. Environmental Protection Agency's guidelines on pesticides and food, pesticides may hurt children by blocking the absorption of vital nutrients essential for normal growth. These chemicals are particularly dangerous during critical periods of development when exposure to toxins can permanently alter the way a human being's biological system operates. Infants and toddlers are thought to be especially vulnerable to these health risks because their internal organs are still in the process of maturing. Also, kids eat and drink more than adults in relation to their body weight, possibly magnifying their exposure to pesticides and other chemicals.

The Dirty Dozen and the Clean Fifteen

The Dirty Dozen are foods that have high levels of pesticide residues when conventionally grown. In 2014, the EWG recommended buying the organic versions of the following (or foregoing them):

- Apples
- Celery
- Cherry tomatoes
- Cucumbers
- Grapes
- Nectarines
- Peaches
- Potatoes
- Snap peas
- Spinach
- Strawberries
- Sweet bell peppers

The Clean Fifteen were found to have the lowest amounts of pesticide contamination in 2014, and are considered safe to buy conventionally grown (that is, nonorganic):

- Asparagus
- Avocados
- Cabbage
- Cantaloupe (domestic)
- Cauliflower
- Eggplant
- Grapefruit
- Kiwis
- Mangos
- Onions
- Papayas
- Pineapples
- Sweet corn
- Sweet peas (frozen)
- Sweet potatoes

In 2012, the American Academy of Pediatrics released its own report on children's exposure to pesticides, citing research that linked pesticide exposure in early life to some pediatric cancers, decreased cognitive function, and behavioral problems.

Even if you make the decision to feed your baby mostly pesticide-free foods, some organic products aren't always available or cost-effective. To help shoppers make informed decisions about when it's absolutely necessary to buy organic produce and when it's okay to settle for conventional, the Environmental Working Group (EWG) releases two lists annually: "The Dirty Dozen" and "The Clean Fifteen."

FRESH, FROZEN, OR CANNED?

Wondering how to choose among fresh, frozen, and canned foods? Theoretically, fresh is the best—but not, as previously noted, when produce is picked too early and shipped across several states (or even oceans) to reach your table. In those cases, frozen fruits and veggies provide a surprisingly nutritious alternative. FDA guidelines released in 2002 not only confirmed that frozen produce is just as nourishing as fresh, it also noted that fruits and vegetables meant for freezing are picked at peak ripeness, blanched, and frozen within mere hours of harvesting, locking in optimal levels of vitamins and minerals.

Canned produce is processed differently from frozen, and the canning process can sometimes deplete nutritional value. Foods are still picked at peak ripeness, but tend to lose some of their vitamin C due to the high temperatures used for canning. Still, according to the American Dietetic Association, some canned vegetables (such as tomatoes, corn, and carrots) actually provide higher levels of antioxidants than their fresh counterparts.

When purchasing canned produce, be sure to avoid varieties with added salt and stick to non-GMO (genetically modified organism) brands when possible. GMOs are combinations of different species of plants or animals that can't occur in nature or by traditional crossbreeding. While GMO consumption has been deemed safe by the FDA, groups such as the Organic Consumers Association, the American Academy of Environmental Medicine, and the Institute for Responsible Technology warn that it has been linked to side effects including allergies and infertility. By buying organic, you can be sure that your purchase does not contain GMOs.

Also steer clear of cans containing bisphenol A (BPA) whenever possible. A common chemical found in the lining of metal food cans and numerous other household products, BPA can disrupt the hormone system, particularly when exposure occurs in infancy or early childhood.

SUPERFOODS

Chances are, you've heard the buzz about "superfoods" and how they should be a part of everyone's diet, but what makes these foods so super—especially for kids? Think of superfoods as turbo-powered produce: fruits and vegetables that not only provide your baby with the nutrition he needs to grow, but also with the disease-preventing antioxidants and healthy fats he needs to thrive. Here are 9 superfoods to include in your little one's daily meals.

Avocados: High in protein and mono-unsaturated fat, avocados may help reduce the risk of heart disease, diabetes, and cancer. They're also high in the antioxidant lutein, which plays an important role in skin and eye health.

Bananas: A great source of potassium, carbohydrates, and fiber, bananas help ease digestion and maintain healthy blood pressure.

Berries: Packed with fiber and vitamins A and C, blueberries, raspberries, and strawberries all boast high levels of immune system–boosting antioxidants.

Broccoli: A cruciferous vegetable known for its cancer-preventing properties, broccoli also delivers generous amounts of beta-carotene, calcium, fiber, folate, and vitamin C.

Butternut squash: Like broccoli, butternut squash is high in beta-carotene, vitamin C, fiber, and folate, plus potassium and certain B vitamins.

Carrots: Your grandma wasn't kidding when she said eating your carrots would help your eyes! These root veggies are bursting with beta-carotene, which converts to vitamin A and supports vision.

Kiwi fruit: In addition to containing vitamin E, thought to protect against the damage caused by free radicals, a single kiwi provides a generous amount of vitamin C, plus plenty of potassium and fiber.

Quinoa: This is one of the most nutritious whole foods available; it's high in protein, fiber, and iron, as well as zinc, selenium, and vitamin E.

Spinach: In addition to vitamin C, beta-carotene, and lutein, this leafy green contains almost twice the daily requirement of vitamin K, which promotes cardiovascular and bone health.

SUPERFOODS

clockwise from top left:

avocados

bananas

berries

broccoli

butternut squash

carrots

kiwi fruit

quinoa

spinach

BUYING LOCALLY GROWN

Another great way to make sure you're getting the most out of your groceries is to search for locally grown and produced foods. When you shop at farmers' markets and in the "local" section of your supermarket, you're buying the freshest produce available, picked hours before delivery instead of days. When fruits and vegetables are shipped long distances, they're exposed to extreme temperatures, light, and other conditions that can cause important nutrients such as vitamins A and C and thiamine (vitamin B_1) to be depleted. Plus, produce meant for traveling is often picked before it has a chance to ripen completely and develop full nutritional potency. Depending on the time of year and weather conditions, however, the fresh fruits and vegetables you're looking for might not always be available. In those cases, frozen or canned produce can be perfectly suitable substitutions.

ALLERGY AWARENESS

According to the Centers for Disease Control and Prevention's "Food Allergies in Schools" report, 4.6 percent of children younger than 18 years of age have a food allergy. An allergic reaction is what happens when your child's body perceives a certain food as a "threat" and her immune system launches an "attack." Symptoms of

Potential Choking Hazards

If your baby shows an interest in finger foods before the age of one, feel free to begin this fun (and messy) phase—but be sure to stay away from these potential choking hazards:

Hot dogs or sausages (unless cut into noodle-like strips and then again into ½-inch chunks)

Whole grapes (okay if chopped in half)

Cherry tomatoes (tomatoes of any size usually aren't introduced until after baby's first birthday because of their acidity)

Popcorn

Chunks of hard cheese (okay if chopped into very small pieces)

White bread (unlike whole-grain bread, white bread can be very mushy and can stick to the roof of baby's mouth and back of his throat, making it difficult to swallow)

Raisins and other sticky, dried fruits

Hard, raw vegetables such as carrots, apples, celery, broccoli, and cauliflower

Common Allergenic and Gassy Foods

Whether or not you have a family history of allergies, it's always a good idea to introduce new foods slowly, waiting four to seven days between the introduction of each unfamiliar item and watching for signs of allergy (such as a runny nose, rash, hives, diarrhea, or trouble breathing). The following eight foods are most likely to cause allergic reactions:

- Cow's milk
- Eggs
- Fish
- Peanuts
- Shellfish
- Soy
- Tree nuts
- Wheat

Sometimes it's tough to tell whether your baby's tummy troubles are the result of an allergy or simply an unfortunate side effect of a certain dish. These 10 foods, while not highly allergenic, have been known to cause gas in babies:

- Apricots
- Beans
- Broccoli
- Brussels sprouts
- Cabbage
- Cauliflower
- Citrus fruits
- Garlic
- Onions
- Prunes

an allergic reaction can range from watery, itchy eyes to hives to vomiting to difficulty breathing. These symptoms usually appear within minutes to two hours of eating a food and can be life-threatening. Other food allergy symptoms, such as gastrointestinal disturbances and rashes, can be chronic.

Delaying Foods Does Not Prevent Allergies

For decades, experts recommended waiting until at least age one to introduce commonly allergenic foods such as eggs, nuts, and fish—but in 2008 the American Academy of Pediatrics released a report ("Effects of Early Nutritional Interventions on the Development of Atopic Disease in Infants and Children") that showed no evidence that delaying the introduction of these foods past four to six months of age prevents food allergies. In fact, guidelines released by the American Academy of Asthma, Allergy and Immunology (AAAI) in 2013 stated that delaying the introduction of foods like wheat, cow's-milk dairy, eggs, nuts, and fish may actually result in an *increased* risk of food allergies. According to the AAAI recommendations, once a baby over four months of age tolerates a few nonallergenic solids such as rice cereal, bananas, sweet potatoes, and apples, parents can move on to feeding foods that are commonly considered to be more allergenic. (Exclusive breastfeeding for the first four months may protect against cow's-milk allergy.)

However, if you have a family history of food allergies or your baby exhibits signs of an allergy, such as eczema, it's best to talk to your family doctor before moving ahead with potentially problematic fare.

CLEANLINESS AND SAFETY

Infants are particularly susceptible to foodborne illnesses, so it's especially important to take the proper precautionary measures when cooking for your child. Babies and toddlers are also known to put too much food in their mouths at one time and try to swallow it before chewing thoroughly (if at all!). Here are some basic tips to help keep your baby safe and healthy at mealtime:

- Always be sure to wash your hands and any equipment used for cooking thoroughly with hot, soapy water. Take apart grinders, blenders, and baby food cookers after each use and wash them well, making sure all the pieces are dry before reassembling.

- Use separate cutting boards for meat and nonmeat foods.

- Cook meat, poultry, and fish thoroughly to kill bacteria. The FDA's Office of Food Safety recommends cooking red meats to an internal temperature of at least 160°F, pork and fish to at least 145°F, and all white meat poultry to an internal temperature of at least 165°F.

- Wash, scrub, or peel all fruits and vegetables, and remove seeds or pits.

- Always grind seeds and nuts.

- Throw away any uneaten leftovers from your baby's dish. Bacteria can grow on uneaten food and pose a risk.

- To prevent choking, make sure your child is seated and supervised during every meal.

- Cut finger foods into pieces no larger than ¼ inch, and serve only a few pieces at a time.

- Sign up for first aid and CPR classes (offered by most hospitals) so that you know how to help your child in an emergency situation.

A WORD ON DESSERT

There's no question that kids of all ages love dessert. But as much as your little one might delight in a bowl of ice cream or a cupcake after dinner, kids benefit most when their sweet tooth is satisfied by naturally sweet foods such as fruit. These days, it's

Foods to Avoid Before Year One

While parents might choose to hold off on some foods due to allergy fears, there is a short list of foods that all babies should avoid for the first year because they pose serious health risks.

Honey: Honey may contain spores of *Clostridium botulinum*, which causes botulism. While an adult's intestinal tract can handle these spores in small amounts, in babies, the spores can grow and produce fatal toxins.

Cow's milk: According to the American Academy of Pediatrics' Committee on Nutrition ("The Use of Cow's Milk in Infancy"), the consumption of cow's milk under one year of age can lead to allergies and/or iron-deficient anemia. For these reasons, you should stick to breast milk or formula for at least the first year.

Low-fat dairy products: Unlike grown-ups, children under the age of two need the fat from dairy products for healthy brain development, according to the University of Minnesota's Academic Health Center. When you introduce dairy to your baby, make sure it's full fat, even if you typically opt for a lower-fat version for

yourself. Just be mindful that although dairy as a category shouldn't be avoided before your baby turns one, cow's milk should.

Undercooked meat and eggs: Babies are more vulnerable than adults to bacteria such as salmonella, which can be present in raw and rare meat, poultry, and eggs. Make sure to cook meat and eggs well before serving them to babies.

Foods to Avoid Adding

Salt: Babies get the salt they need naturally from foods; there is no need to add more, as adults tend to do for themselves to flavor meals. According to the global group World Action on Salt & Health (WASH), babies require very small amounts of sodium; in fact, their kidneys are too immature to cope with any added salt. After 12 months, WASH recommends a maximum of 2 grams per day.

Sugar: Added sugar can wreak havoc on brand-new teeth. Plus, it fills up little tummies with empty calories, leaving less room for the nutritious food babies really need.

easy to find bags of organic, frozen chunks of fruit such as mango or pineapple in the grocery store. It only takes a few moments to let them thaw before you can slice them up and serve them to your child. These raw fruits burst with flavor, and little ones tend to appreciate their coldness, too, during the teething months.

Of course, an occasional cup of ice cream or cookie is fine—little indulgences are not going to compromise a lifetime of good health. But you won't find a chapter dedicated to desserts for little ones in this book. However, there is an appendix that includes five homemade and delicious treats meant for celebrating your baby's first birthday—an event so special it's worth breaking the rules! Remember, it's all about instilling healthy habits, and moderation is the key to success.

CHAPTER TWO

Fast and Easy Cooking

· ·

While it's true that there's no faster way to get a meal on the table (or high chair tray) than by merely opening a jar, preparing your baby's food from scratch doesn't have to take much longer. In roughly the time it takes to make yourself a sandwich, you can whip up a fresh, healthy treat for your little one that tastes a million times better than any prepackaged option ever could—and this book will show you how.

Unfortunately, some absolutely wonderful foods for babies are impossible to cook in just a handful of minutes (unless you use the microwave). Because this book focuses on both fresh *and* fast meals, you won't find recipes in these pages that include stove-cooked or oven-roasted ingredients such as fresh beets, white potatoes, or winter squash (though some of these foods make an appearance in their canned or frozen forms). In some cases, there are tips and tricks provided for cooking these items more quickly than usual, for example, by cutting them into very small pieces before steaming or roasting.

Don't worry if you're not an experienced chef—you can still be an efficient one, particularly when it comes to cooking for your little one. After all, infants and toddlers don't require four-course gourmet feasts! Once you get into the habit of making your own baby food, you'll become more and more competent in the kitchen.

COOKING METHODS FOR ALL

There's no need to master the art of deglazing or find out how to properly flambé; the techniques you'll need to learn in order to prepare the recipes in these chapters are relatively simple. In fact, you're probably already familiar with them.

- **Steaming:** Steaming cooks food by exposing it to steam from continuously boiling water while keeping the food separate from the water in a bamboo or metal steamer (sometimes a metal basket placed in a pot filled with an inch or two of water and sealed with a lid). Preparing food this way preserves the nutrients lost with boiling or, to a lesser degree, simmering.

- **Roasting:** Roasting cooks foods (in this book, vegetables) through an indirect heat source such as an oven. A high level of nutrients is usually retained, as long as the vegetables aren't overcooked, and roasting tends to enhance the flavors of certain foods (sweet potatoes, zucchini, and cauliflower, for example). Roasting vegetables typically involves adding a small amount of some type of fat, such as olive oil, to keep food from sticking to the pan and/or drying out.

- **Baking:** Baking works in much the same way as roasting, but the recipes that call for baking in this book don't require the addition of oils because the foods being cooked already contain fat (meat, eggs, dairy).

- **Sautéing:** Sautéing uses a small amount of oil or fat to cook food over medium to high heat.

TOOLS AND EQUIPMENT

Luckily, most of the utensils and cookware required to prepare your baby's food are likely already in your kitchen. Here are the absolute essential tools you'll need to get started.

- **Stainless-steel steamer basket:** Used for steaming fruits and vegetables, a steamer basket is both inexpensive and indispensable.

- **Blender or food processor:** While both food processors and blenders can be used to make baby food purées and mashes, food processors can also chop, shred, grate, and slice, and are better at mixing and blending hard foods. That said, food processors are also more expensive, and most blenders serve as perfectly adequate baby food makers.

- **Strainer/colander:** You'll need this for rinsing fruits and veggies, as well as draining pastas and other boiled foods.

- **Four-sided box grater:** This is useful not just for grating cheese, but fruits and vegetables, too.

- **Peeler:** A peeler is great for peeling hard vegetables and fruits, including carrots, sweet potatoes, apples, and pears.

- **Ice cube tray:** Whether plastic, stainless steel, or silicone, these trays come in handy for freezing individual portions of baby food.

STORING, THAWING, AND REHEATING

Since your baby will eat only a few tablespoons of food at a time, at least in the beginning, you'll be preparing food that will last you some time. That's why it's so important to know how to correctly store the meals you've prepared—improper storage, thawing, or reheating can cause bacteria to grow that could make your baby sick. Leftovers on your baby's plate should be thrown away.

Storing

Here are some essential tips to become a master of baby food storage, maximizing your time and your budget.

- Let prepared food cool to room temperature before refrigerating or freezing.

- Never allow cooked food to stand at room temperature for more than two hours (or more than one hour if room temperature is above 90°F).

- Ice cube trays are the ultimate in convenience for freezing individual portions. Many parents buy new ice cube trays intentionally and solely for this purpose. After filling the compartments, cover the tray with plastic wrap and freeze until firm, usually about two hours. You can then pop out the frozen portions into a zip-top plastic bag. Make sure to note what the food is (it's not always obvious!) and mark the date, too.

Thawing and Reheating

Here are some smart strategies for thawing and reheating food.

- Thaw frozen food overnight in the refrigerator—never at room temperature. If you choose to thaw food in the microwave, be sure to stir often and use the defrost setting.

- Reheat food in a pan on the stove, rather than in a microwave, to avoid hot spots.

- Always test the temperature of baby's foods before serving.

- Once you've thawed foods, don't refreeze them. Instead, store them in the refrigerator (for up to two days).

PLANNING AND PREPPING AHEAD

With a little careful planning, you can easily prepare your baby's entire menu for the week in just an hour or two.

1. Start by determining which foods you'll be serving.

2. Make a grocery list that includes all the ingredients in each recipe.

3. Once you have everything you need, sort the items into categories: which need to be steamed, which need to be baked or roasted, and which need to be puréed or chopped without cooking.

4. Get to work making the food assembly-line style: Wash and chop all the ingredients. Steam the first item, remove it from the steamer, and place it in the blender. Put the second item to be steamed in the steamer, and steam while the first item is being puréed, and so on.

5. Cool and freeze all the foods according to the instructions on page 23.

This is also an ideal time to make foods that take longer than 30 minutes to prepare. Are you making a Sunday roast with sweet potatoes for the family? Toss some of the cooked meat and potatoes into the blender or food processor, and store the purée in the freezer for later in the week. Are you making brown rice? Cook a big batch; then purée and freeze individual portions to be served on their own or mixed with other foods.

By approaching meal planning this way, virtually anything can be prepared on the spot in 30 minutes or less.

HOW TO USE THIS BOOK

Throughout the rest of this book, the chapters follow a similar format. Each begins with introductory information covering your child's readiness for various solid foods and textures at that particular age, appropriate serving sizes, how much milk or formula should still be consumed, as well as some more general advice. Each chapter also includes a chart of new foods that can be introduced and at which month.

Following the introductory information, each chapter offers numerous recipes. With every recipe, you'll find various labels and icons. These labels will help you to find certain types of recipes more quickly:

- **Freezer:** This recipe can be frozen for a significant length of time.

- **Superfood:** This recipe contains a superfood.

- **Dietary labels:** These will tell you whether recipes are one or more of the following:

  - gluten-free
  - nut-free
  - dairy-free
  - vegetarian
  - vegan

This book does not specify "organic" in its ingredient lists, but it's recommended that you do buy pesticide-free, hormone-free fruits, vegetables, dairy products, and meats as often as you can for your growing little one. For easy reference, turn to page 12 for a list of the Dirty Dozen and Clean Fifteen fruits and vegetables.

Smooth Introductions

· ·

No longer a newborn, your baby will make huge developmental leaps between the ages of four and six months. Instead of just flailing his arms and legs aimlessly, he'll begin kicking and squirming more purposefully (to flip himself over from his tummy to his back, for example), and his growing muscle strength will give him better control over his head and neck. At six months old, many babies are able to sit up unassisted and some are even starting to creep or crawl. Vision and hand-eye coordination are also improving, making it possible for babies to reach out and grasp toys and whatever else they see.

IS BABY READY?

After months of exclusively bottle feeding or breastfeeding your baby, you're probably eager to introduce solid foods—but how do you know if he's ready to make the switch? These signs of readiness will help you make the right decision at the right time:

- Your baby can keep his head in an upright position without wobbling and can sit upright while supported.

- He's able to move food to the back of his mouth and swallow it, and doesn't use his tongue to push food out of his mouth.

- He seems hungry even though he's getting the required amount of breast milk or formula per day.

- He shows interest in what you're eating, maybe even reaching out for your fork.

RECOMMENDED SERVING SIZES

The key to successfully introducing your baby to solids is starting slowly—no more than 1 teaspoon of puréed food mixed with 4 to 5 teaspoons of breast milk or formula per day at first, increasing to twice a day. By the six months mark, you can begin to add in oatmeal or rice cereal; gradually increase the thickness of the cereal by mixing it with less liquid.

BREAST MILK OR FORMULA

Remember, your baby still depends on breast milk or formula for almost all of his nutritional needs, so you should continue to feed him 24 to 32 ounces of breast milk or formula in a 24-hour period (usually between eight and ten feedings a day if breastfeeding).

SPILLS AND SETBACKS

Just because babies on TV commercials eagerly slurp up whatever's offered to them on a spoon doesn't mean real-life mealtimes will be quite so picture-perfect. Don't be surprised if the first few—or few dozen—times you offer solids, your baby's reaction is to promptly spit them out. Some babies even shudder at the foreign tastes and textures! These refusals (and the resulting messes) are perfectly normal. Throughout this sloppy and sometimes silly process, keep the following advice in mind:

- Don't automatically assume your baby will never like a certain dish just because he doesn't seem to at first. Some infants and toddlers need to try a new food up to 10 times before accepting it.

- While some pediatricians recommend introducing veggies before fruit so that a baby's palate won't be "spoiled" for more bitter tastes, this rule isn't set in stone. Some babies need their veggies mixed with fruit at first in order to get used to the flavor.

- Remember to laugh. Sure, you're tired and frustrated and have a huge mess on your hands, but someday you'll remember that little applesauce-covered face and smile.

NEW FOODS TO INTRODUCE

At four months:

Apples	Avocados	Green beans
Apricots	Bananas	Pears
Asparagus	Butternut squash	Sweet potatoes

At six months:

Carrots	Nectarines	Plums	Quinoa
Mangos	Parsnips	Prunes	Rice
Oatmeal	Peas	Pumpkin	Zucchini

Cooked Fruit Purées

GLUTEN-FREE **NUT-FREE** DAIRY-FREE VEGAN

PREP TIME: 5 MINUTES • COOK TIME: 5 TO 10 MINUTES

Purées made from cooked fruits are among almost every baby's very first tastes of solid food. Cooking fruit before puréeing it will give it a smoother consistency and, in some cases, help make it easier for baby to digest. Plus, having a variety of cooked fruit purées in the freezer means you'll always be able to sweeten up cereals, veggies, and even meats at a moment's notice.

Most of the fruits on this list should be peeled before cooking, particularly apples, pears, and peaches; in the beginning, you might want to peel all of your baby's fruits, as skins can be difficult for novice tummies to process. Cores and pits should be removed, and the fruit's flesh should be cut into chunks.

	AMOUNT	COOKING TIME	MAKES
Apples	1 large apple	8 minutes	⅔ cup
Apricots	2 medium apricots	5 minutes	½ cup
Nectarines	1 medium nectarine	5 minutes	⅓ cup
Peaches	1 medium peach	5 minutes	½ cup
Pears	1 large pear	5 minutes	⅔ cup
Plums	1 large plum/pluot	5 minutes	⅓ cup
Prunes	½ cup prunes	10 minutes	¼ cup

1. Fill a medium saucepan with about 1 inch of water and bring to a simmer.

2. Place the fruit in a steamer basket, set it over the simmering water, cover, and cook until tender when pierced with a fork, 5 to 10 minutes, depending on the type of fruit.

3. Remove the pan from the heat and let the fruit cool, reserving the steaming liquid.

4. When the fruit has cooled, transfer it to either a blender or food processor and purée (or transfer the fruit to a bowl and purée using an immersion blender). For a thinner consistency, add some of the reserved steaming liquid, water, breast milk, or formula. Cooked fruit can also be mashed with a fork when baby is ready for thicker, chunkier textures.

PREPARING PRUNES. Unlike the other fruits on this list, prunes should be stewed instead of steamed. Put ½ cup of chopped prunes into a saucepan with 1½ cups of water and bring to a boil over medium-high heat. Simmer for about 10 minutes, or until tender. Remove from the heat and pour through a fine-mesh strainer, reserving the cooking liquid. Set aside to cool. Purée the cooled prunes in a blender or food processor, adding the reserved cooking liquid as necessary to reach the desired consistency.

STORAGE: Refrigerate leftover purée in an airtight container for up to 3 days or freeze for up to 3 months.

NOTES

Raw Fruit Purées

GLUTEN-FREE **NUT-FREE** DAIRY-FREE VEGAN

PREP TIME: 5 MINUTES

Preparing raw fruit purées couldn't be easier. If the fruit you've chosen is ripe and soft enough, you won't even need a blender—a fork will suffice! This simple method makes raw fruit purée a perfect choice when you're on the go (or just busy at home). At six months, feel free to add peaches and nectarines to the following list.

	AMOUNT	MAKES
Avocados*	1 medium avocado	½ cup
Bananas*	1 large banana	⅓ cup
Mangos	1 large mango	½ cup

Superfood

1. Peel the fruit. If you're using mango, cut the fruit in half lengthwise as close to the pit as possible and pull apart. Slice the flesh of the mango into small squares (don't cut all the way through the skin). Pop the squares out by pushing from the skin side, and cut the cubes off.

2. If you're using avocado, slice the fruit in half lengthwise the same way you would a mango, pull the halves apart, remove the pit with a knife or spoon, and then scoop the flesh out. Purée the fruit in a blender or food processor (or mash it with a fork, if it's soft enough). Mix with water, breast milk, or formula if necessary.

STORAGE: Refrigerate leftover purée in an airtight container for up to 3 days or freeze for up to 3 months.

NOTES

Steamed Vegetable Purées

GLUTEN-FREE **NUT-FREE** DAIRY-FREE VEGAN

PREP TIME: 5 MINUTES • COOK TIME: 5 TO 15 MINUTES

Steaming is the easiest, quickest way to bring out the flavor of fresh—or even frozen— vegetables. It may seem strange at first to serve your baby veggies without any salt, dressings, or sauces, since most adults prefer their vegetables with these additions, but you'll soon discover that baby's palate is perfectly primed for these straight-from-the-garden treats.

	AMOUNT	COOKING TIME	MAKES
Asparagus	1 medium bunch asparagus	8 minutes	2½ cups
Carrots*	2 medium carrots	8 minutes	⅔ cup
Green beans	1 cup green beans	8 minutes	⅓ cup
Peas	1 cup peas	5 minutes	½ cup
Sweet potatoes	1 medium sweet potato	15 minutes	⅔ cup
Zucchini	1 medium zucchini	8 minutes	½ cup

Superfood

1. Wash, peel, and trim the vegetables as needed. If using asparagus or green beans, be sure to trim and discard the ends; carrots, sweet potatoes, and zucchini should be peeled. Cut large vegetables into smaller pieces; the smaller the pieces, the shorter the cooking time.

2. Fill a medium saucepan with about 1 inch of water and bring to a simmer. Place the vegetables in a steamer basket, set it over the simmering water, cover, and cook until tender when pierced with a fork, 5 to 10 minutes, depending on the type of vegetable; sweet potatoes might take 12 to 15 minutes.

(Continued)

3. Remove the pan from the heat and let the veggies cool, reserving the steaming liquid. When the vegetables have cooled, purée in either a blender or food processor (or transfer to a bowl and purée using an immersion blender). For a thinner consistency, add some of the reserved steaming liquid, water, breast milk, or formula.

STORAGE: Refrigerate leftover purée in an airtight container for up to 3 days or freeze for up to 3 months.

NOTES

Cereals

NUT-FREE DAIRY-FREE **GLUTEN-FREE** VEGAN

PREP TIME: 5 MINUTES • COOK TIME: 10 MINUTES

Traditionally, most pediatricians recommended rice cereal as a first food for babies, before even bananas or applesauce. The advice in recent years has changed, liberating parents to begin with more flavorful vegetables and fruits. While first cereals can be pretty bland, babies tend to be fans, especially of oatmeal. Oats do not contain the gluten protein, but they can be cross-contaminated with gluten when processed in factories with other gluten-containing foods. Opt for oats labeled gluten-free.

As a reminder, cereals should not be introduced before the age of 6 months.

	AMOUNT	COOKING TIME	MAKES
Brown rice	¼ cup	10 minutes	¾ cup
Oats	¼ cup	10 minutes	¾ cup
Quinoa	¼ cup	10 minutes	¾ cup

1. In a blender or food processor, grind the grain until it reaches a powdery consistency. (This will take longer for brown rice and quinoa than for oats.)

2. In a saucepan, bring 1 cup of water to a boil over high heat. Add the grain and reduce the heat to low. Simmer for 10 minutes, whisking continuously, until all of the liquid has been absorbed.

3. Pour the cereal into a bowl and serve as is, or mix with fruit, veggie, or (when your baby is older) meat purée.

STORAGE: Refrigerate leftover cereal in an airtight container for up to 3 days or freeze for up to 3 months.

NOTES

Green Beans and Pear Purée

MAKES 8 SERVINGS, ¼ CUP EACH
PREP TIME: 8 MINUTES • COOK TIME: 8 MINUTES

High in calcium and vitamin K, green beans are a great nutrient-dense first vegetable for your baby—and mixing them with sweet, tasty pears makes a spoonful go down easily. Plus, pears are packed with fiber and vitamin C and are known for being especially gentle on little tummies, making them a perfect choice for babies who might be suffering from reflux.

Tip: *If you're pressed for time and want to skip the trimming step, frozen green beans can be used in a pinch. In fact, frozen beans, which tend to be less tough, will make the texture of this purée even smoother.*

1 large pear, peeled and cored   1 cup trimmed fresh green beans

1. Chop the pear into 1-inch cubes.

2. Fill a medium saucepan with about 1 inch of water and bring to a simmer. Place the green beans and pear in a steamer basket, set it over the simmering water, cover, and cook until the green beans and pear are tender when pierced with a fork, about 8 minutes. Allow to cool.

3. In a blender or food processor, purée the green beans and pear until smooth. Add water if necessary to achieve the desired consistency.

STORAGE: Leftover purée can be refrigerated in an airtight container for up to 2 days or frozen for up to 3 months.

NOTES _____

_____

_____

_____

Apple and Mango Purée

GLUTEN-FREE **NUT-FREE** DAIRY-FREE VEGAN

MAKES 4 SERVINGS, ¼ CUP EACH
PREP TIME: 8 MINUTES • COOK TIME: 8 MINUTES

Sure, every baby loves applesauce, but why not make it more exciting with the addition of tropical mangos? Higher in carotenoids (said to fight cancer, heart disease, and even the common cold) than almost any other fruit, mangos give plain old applesauce an irresistibly tangy taste. Nearly any type of apple works well in this recipe, though babies tend to prefer the sweetness of Red or Golden Delicious, Gala, and Empire apples.

Tip: *Look for mangos that are slightly soft and smell sweet, with no bruises or brown dots. They should be reddish-orange or golden reddish-orange in color. Avoid mangos that are too soft, as they can be stringy in texture when overly ripe.*

1 large apple, peeled and cored

1 large mango, peeled and cubed (see page 32)

1. Chop the apple into 1-inch chunks.

2. Fill a medium saucepan with about 1 inch of water and bring to a simmer. Place the apple in a steamer basket, set it over the simmering water, cover, and cook until tender, about 8 minutes. Allow to cool.

3. In a blender or food processor, purée the cooled apple and the mango until smooth. Add water if necessary to achieve the desired consistency.

STORAGE: Leftover purée can be refrigerated in an airtight container for up to 2 days or frozen for up to 3 months.

NOTES

Avocado and Banana Purée

SUPERFOOD GLUTEN-FREE **NUT-FREE** DAIRY-FREE VEGAN

MAKES 4 SERVINGS, ¼ CUP EACH
PREP TIME: 10 MINUTES

The combined creaminess of avocados and bananas makes this purée a particularly rich treat. High in potassium, bananas also provide vitamins B₂, B₆, and C. Avocados are loaded with healthy fats and folic acid, and help the body absorb fat-soluble nutrients such as beta-carotene and lutein. Both avocados and bananas are especially mild in flavor, making this a good first choice for sensitive palates.

Tip: *Look for avocados that are extremely dark green (almost black) in color and slightly soft. If all of the avocados at the store are hard, unripe avocados can be left to ripen on your kitchen counter for a day or so.*

1 large avocado, halved and pitted (see page 32)

1 large banana, peeled

1. Cut the avocado and banana into 1-inch chunks.

2. Using a fork, mash the chunks together until you reach a relatively smooth consistency. Add water as necessary to thin the mash.

3. Alternatively, to ensure a very smooth consistency, put the avocado and banana in a blender or food processor, and purée until smooth.

STORAGE: Leftover purée can be refrigerated in an airtight container for up to 2 days.

NOTES

Peas and Carrots Purée

SUPERFOOD   GLUTEN-FREE   **NUT-FREE**   DAIRY-FREE   VEGAN

MAKES 8 SERVINGS, ¼ CUP EACH
COOK TIME: 5 MINUTES

Nothing goes together better than peas and carrots, and both bring a variety of essential nutrients to the table. Carrots are high in vitamin A, vitamin C, and calcium; peas are packed with folate and iron. Both have mellow, sweet flavors that are popular with most babies. But the best part about this recipe is that it calls for frozen veggies, making it a snap to prepare.

Variation: *Make this mix even sweeter by adding fresh banana chunks. Other fruit purées, such as apple or pear, also work well, but bananas add a welcome creaminess to these veggies.*

1 (10-ounce) bag frozen mixed peas
  and carrots

1. Fill a medium saucepan with about 1 inch of water and bring to a simmer. Place the vegetables in a steamer basket, set it over the simmering water, cover, and cook until tender, about 5 minutes. Allow to cool.

2. In a blender or food processor, purée the cooled peas and carrots until smooth. Add water if necessary to achieve the desired consistency.

STORAGE: Leftover purée can be refrigerated in an airtight container for up to 2 days or frozen for up to 3 months.

NOTES

Plum and Nectarine Purée

GLUTEN-FREE **NUT-FREE** DAIRY-FREE VEGAN

MAKES 4 SERVINGS, ¼ CUP EACH
PREP TIME: 5 MINUTES • COOK TIME: 5 MINUTES

Since both of these tangy, tasty fruits are high in fiber, this combo makes a great digestive aid for your baby. Plums and nectarines are also great sources of vitamins C and A. After your baby reaches seven months of age, leave the skins on for extra fiber and nutrition; younger babies might have a hard time digesting the whole fruit.

Tip: *Black or red plums work equally well in this recipe. Look for black plums that have dark skins with a flush of purple or red; red plums should be firm and uniform in color. Avoid plums with a brownish tinge to their skin, as these are often mealy in texture.*

1 large plum, pitted and peeled   1 medium nectarine, pitted and peeled

1. Cut the plum and nectarine into 1-inch chunks.

2. Fill a medium saucepan with about 1 inch of water and bring to a simmer. Place the plum and nectarine in a steamer basket, set it over the simmering water, cover, and cook until tender, about 5 minutes. Allow to cool.

3. In a blender or food processor, purée the cooled plum and nectarine until smooth. Add water if necessary to achieve the desired consistency.

   STORAGE: Leftover purée can be refrigerated in an airtight container for up to 2 days or frozen for up to 3 months.

   NOTES _____

   _____

   _____

   _____

Carrot and Mango Purée

SUPERFOOD GLUTEN-FREE NUT-FREE DAIRY-FREE VEGAN

MAKES 6 SERVINGS, ¼ CUP EACH
PREP TIME: 5 MINUTES • COOK TIME: 8 MINUTES

The lovely orange hue of this mellow mix is sure to catch baby's eye and the beta-carotene will help make his eyes strong. Think of this as a tropical smoothie on a spoon. Bananas make a great addition if you happen to have one on hand; once baby reaches seven or eight months, consider tossing in some fresh kiwi or papaya. When you're ready to introduce dairy, mix this purée with plain, full-fat yogurt.

Tip: *Frozen carrots can be used in place of fresh carrots in this recipe if you don't have time for peeling and chopping. An added bonus to using frozen carrots is their slightly less pungent flavor, which babies sometimes prefer.*

1 medium carrot, peeled

1 large mango, peeled and cut into cubes (see page 32)

1. Cut the carrot into small rounds.

2. Fill a medium saucepan with about 1 inch of water and bring to a simmer. Place the carrot in a steamer basket, set it over the simmering water, cover, and cook until tender, about 8 minutes. Allow to cool.

3. In a blender or food processor, purée the cooled carrot and the mango until smooth. Add water if necessary to achieve the desired consistency.

STORAGE: Leftover purée can be refrigerated in an airtight container for up to 2 days or frozen for up to 3 months.

NOTES

Sweet Potato and Green Beans Purée

GLUTEN-FREE · **NUT-FREE** · **DAIRY-FREE** · **VEGAN**

MAKES 8 SERVINGS, ¼ CUP EACH

PREP TIME: 8 MINUTES • COOK TIME: 10 TO 15 MINUTES

Sweet potatoes (or yams, which are very similar but not the same vegetable—though your baby won't know!) are a surefire hit with almost all babies and are great for mixing with (and masking the taste of) almost any other vegetable. They're also particularly high in vitamins A and C, folate, iron, copper, and calcium. While baking sweet potatoes takes longer than 30 minutes, cutting these root veggies into small pieces makes it possible to steam them in less than 15 minutes.

Tip: *Fresh green beans can be replaced with frozen, and fresh sweet potato can be replaced with unsweetened canned sweet potato purée or canned/frozen butternut squash purée.*

1 medium sweet potato, peeled   1 cup trimmed fresh green beans

1. Cut the sweet potato into ½-inch chunks.

2. Fill a medium saucepan with about 1 inch of water and bring to a simmer. Place the sweet potato and green beans in a steamer basket, set it over the simmering water, cover, and cook until tender, 10 to 15 minutes. The green beans may cook more quickly and can be removed first. Allow the vegetables to cool.

3. In a blender or food processor, purée the cooled sweet potato and green beans until smooth. Add water if necessary to achieve the desired consistency.

STORAGE: Leftover purée can be refrigerated in an airtight container for up to 2 days or frozen for up to 3 months.

NOTES ————————————————————————

————————————————————————————————

————————————————————————————————

Avocado and Pear Purée

SUPERFOOD   GLUTEN-FREE   **NUT-FREE**   DAIRY-FREE   VEGAN

MAKES 6 SERVINGS, ¼ CUP EACH
PREP TIME: 5 MINUTES • COOK TIME: 5 MINUTES

Two of the most palatable early foods for "picky" eaters, avocados and pears make it easy being green. Sweet and refreshing, this dish has universal appeal and is a great base for mixing with cereals and other puréed veggies, fruits, and cereals (particularly rice and quinoa). Try it with peas or apples.

Tip: *When choosing pears, keep in mind that Anjou and Bartlett tend to be less mealy than Bosc (though Bosc are usually the sweetest). After a few "experiments," you'll definitely be able to figure out which variety your baby prefers!*

1 ripe avocado, halved and pitted (see page 32)

1 large pear, peeled and cored

1. Chop the avocado and pear into 1-inch chunks.

2. Fill a medium saucepan with about 1 inch of water and bring to a simmer. Place the pear in a steamer basket, set it over the simmering water, cover, and cook until tender, about 5 minutes. Allow to cool.

3. In a blender or food processor, purée the cooled pear and the avocado until smooth. Add water if necessary to achieve the desired consistency.

STORAGE: Leftover purée can be refrigerated in an airtight container for up to 2 days.

NOTES

Zucchini and Banana Purée

SUPERFOOD   GLUTEN-FREE   NUT-FREE   DAIRY-FREE   VEGAN

MAKES 4 SERVINGS, ¼ CUP EACH
PREP TIME: 5 MINUTES • COOK TIME: 5 MINUTES

Due to their mild taste and soft texture, zucchini and yellow squash blend well with most other fruits and veggies. They're also high in potassium and vitamins A, C, and K, and even have small amounts of selenium, copper, and manganese. Due to their high water content, purées made with these summer squash tend not to need any added liquids. Bananas do a nice job of balancing out the watery quality of summer squash.

Tip: *Look for zucchini that are smaller in diameter, as these are usually sweeter. Look for yellow squash without brown spots or blemishes, which can indicate an unpleasantly spongy consistency.*

1 medium zucchini or yellow squash, peeled

1 large banana, peeled

1. Cut the zucchini into 1-inch chunks.

2. Fill a medium saucepan with about 1 inch of water and bring to a simmer. Place the zucchini in a steamer basket, set it over the simmering water, cover, and cook until tender, about 5 minutes. Allow to cool.

3. While the zucchini is steaming, cut the banana into 1-inch chunks.

4. In a blender or food processor, purée the banana and cooled zucchini until smooth. Add water if necessary to achieve the desired consistency.

STORAGE: Leftover purée can be refrigerated in an airtight container for up to 2 days or frozen for up to 3 months.

NOTES

Apple, Nectarine, and Banana Purée

SUPERFOOD · GLUTEN-FREE · NUT-FREE · DAIRY-FREE · VEGAN

MAKES 6 SERVINGS, ¼ CUP EACH
PREP TIME: 5 MINUTES · COOK TIME: 5 MINUTES

This fruit salad in purée form offers such a pleasing balance of flavors, older kids and grown-ups will be tempted to sneak some from baby's plate! The banana adds a pleasant thickness to the more watery textures of the apple and nectarine, and the nectarine brings an intriguing tang to the mix. At seven or eight months, or whenever you decide to introduce dairy to your baby's diet, try adding full-fat yogurt.

Tip: *When choosing nectarines, look for fruit that's slightly soft and fragrant, without any hint of green on the skin. Also try to avoid nectarines that appear overly waxy. If nectarines are out of season, try replacing them with frozen peaches, which will give this purée a fluffier texture.*

1 large apple, peeled and cored

1 large banana, peeled

1 medium nectarine, pitted and peeled

1. Cut the apple and nectarine into 1-inch chunks.

2. Fill a medium saucepan with about 1 inch of water and bring to a simmer. Place the apple and nectarine in a steamer basket, set it over the simmering water, cover, and cook until tender, about 5 minutes. Allow to cool.

3. While the apple and nectarine are steaming, cut the banana into 1-inch chunks.

4. In a blender or food processor, purée the banana with the cooled apple and nectarine until smooth. Add water if necessary to achieve the desired consistency.

STORAGE: Leftover purée can be refrigerated in an airtight container for up to 2 days or frozen for up to 3 months.

NOTES

New Flavors and Textures

• •

At seven and eight months of age, your baby's motor skills and hand-eye coordination are improving rapidly. Not only can she most likely roll over in both directions, but your little one may also be sitting up on her own, rocking back and forth on her hands and knees, crawling, or even pulling herself to a standing position. She's getting better at transferring objects from one hand to the other, as well as from her hand to her mouth—so if you haven't baby-proofed the house already, now's the time. She's beginning to figure out how to pick things up using just her thumb and forefinger (called the pincer grasp). Baby is also learning to chew by moving her jaw up and down, which replaces the sucking motion.

IS BABY READY?

Most seven- to eight-month-old babies are ready to move on from single-ingredient, smooth purées to combination purées and thicker, mashed meals. You can start combining foods when you've already introduced at least one of the items separately and checked for food allergies. Wait until your baby is sitting up in a high chair unassisted, and try introducing these new menu options at a time when she's not extremely hungry, possibly alternating between bites of a familiar purée and small tastes of the textured food. If she has a problem tolerating the lumps in the textured food (evidenced by gagging or spitting out the food), go back to smoother purées (whether combination or single ingredient) and try again another time.

RECOMMENDED SERVING SIZES

Between seven and eight months of age, your baby should be eating solid foods two or three times a day. Each serving should be about the size of your baby's fist. These servings could include:

- ¼ to ½ cup fruit, spread out over two or three feedings
- ¼ to ½ cup vegetables, spread out over two or three feedings
- 3 to 9 tablespoons cereal such as oatmeal, brown rice, quinoa, or millet, spread out over two or three feedings

BREAST MILK OR FORMULA

Even though solid foods are playing an increasingly larger role in your baby's diet, breastfeeding or bottle feeding still provide the bulk of her nutrition. In addition to her meals, she should be drinking 24 to 32 ounces of breast milk or formula in a 24-hour period.

TRANSITIONING TO A SIPPY CUP

According to the American Academy of Pediatrics' (AAP's) Healthychildren.org, most babies are ready to start drinking from a sippy cup between six and nine months of age. While some babies make the switch from breast or bottle to sippy cup seamlessly, others need a little encouragement (AAP's "Infant Food and Feeding"). Here are some tips to help make the transition easier:

* Stick to filling sippy cups with breast milk, formula, or water, and try to avoid juice, which can lead to tooth decay.

* Start out with a soft spout that feels more like a nipple, as opposed to the hard plastic variety.

* Before offering a sippy cup to your baby for the first time, try dipping the tip of the spout into breast milk or formula.

* Physically demonstrate to your baby how to lift the cup up to his mouth and tip it back to drink.

* Try a variety of models until you find the right fit. Some "no-spill" valves make it very difficult for babies to get a drink; others come with built-in straws, which certain babies seem to prefer.

NEW FOODS TO INTRODUCE

At seven months:

Beef	Cinnamon	Tofu	Yogurt (full-fat)
Chicken	Pork	Turkey	

At eight months:

Beets	Collard greens	Kale	Raspberries
Blueberries	Cranberries	Kamut	Swiss chard
Broccoli	Cucumber	Kiwi	
Buckwheat	Eggplant	Melons	
Cherries	Flax	Millet	

Cooked Fruit Purées

SUPERFOOD　GLUTEN-FREE　**NUT-FREE**　DAIRY-FREE　VEGAN

PREP TIME: 5 MINUTES • COOK TIME: 5 MINUTES

	AMOUNT	COOKING TIME	MAKES
Blueberries	1 cup blueberries	5 minutes	½ cup
Cherries	1 cup cherries	5 minutes	½ cup

1. While cherries and blueberries don't absolutely need to be cooked before puréeing, it's a good idea to steam them first if they're not particularly ripe or sweet. Both should be washed thoroughly. If you're using cherries, remove the stems and slice the fruit in half, working your knife around the pit to remove it.

2. For cherries or blueberries, fill a medium saucepan with about 1 inch of water and bring to a simmer. Place the fruit in a steamer basket, set it over the simmering water, cover, and cook until tender (usually 5 minutes). Remove the pan from the heat and let the fruit cool, reserving the steaming liquid.

3. When the fruit has cooled, purée it in either a blender or food processor (or transfer it to a bowl and purée using an immersion blender). Add the reserved steaming liquid as necessary to achieve the desired consistency.

STORAGE: Refrigerate leftover purée in an airtight container for up to 3 days or freeze for up to 3 months.

NOTES

Raw Fruit Purées

GLUTEN-FREE **NUT-FREE** DAIRY-FREE VEGAN

PREP TIME: 5 MINUTES

	AMOUNT	MAKES
Kiwi*	1 large kiwi	¼ cup
Melon	1 small melon (cantaloupe, honeydew, or seedless watermelon)	1½ cups
Papaya	1 medium papaya	1¼ cups

*Superfood

1. Wash the fruit. Kiwis should be peeled; if you're using papaya or melon, cut the fruit in half and scoop out the seeds, cut the fruit into slices, remove the rind or skin using a sharp knife, and chop the flesh into cubes or chunks.

2. In a blender or food processor, purée the fruit; in the case of kiwi or watermelon, mash with a fork instead for a thicker consistency. Add water, breast milk, or formula if necessary to achieve the desired consistency.

STORAGE: Refrigerate leftover purée in an airtight container for up to 2 days or freeze for up to 3 months.

NOTES

Steamed Vegetable Purées

PREP TIME: 2 MINUTES • COOK TIME: 5 TO 10 MINUTES

	AMOUNT	COOKING TIME	MAKES
Broccoli*	1 small head broccoli (florets only)	5 to 10 minutes	⅔ cup
Cauliflower	1 small head cauliflower (florets only)	5 to 10 minutes	⅔ cup

Superfood

1. Soak the broccoli or cauliflower florets in cold water for 2 minutes, then rinse and pat dry.

2. Fill a medium saucepan with about 1 inch of water and bring to a simmer. Place the vegetables in a steamer basket, set it over the simmering water, cover, and cook until tender when pierced with a fork, 5 to 10 minutes. Remove the pan from the heat and let the veggies cool, reserving the steaming liquid.

3. When the veggies have cooled, purée them in either a blender or food processor (or transfer them to a bowl and purée using an immersion blender). For a thinner consistency, add some of the reserved steaming liquid, water, breast milk, or formula.

STORAGE: Refrigerate leftover purée in an airtight container for up to 2 days or freeze for up to 3 months.

NOTES ——————————————————————————

———————————————————————————————————

———————————————————————————————————

———————————————————————————————————

Sautéed Greens Purées

GLUTEN-FREE   NUT-FREE   DAIRY-FREE   VEGAN

PREP TIME: 5 MINUTES ● COOK TIME: 5 TO 10 MINUTES

	AMOUNT	COOKING TIME	MAKES
Collard greens	1 small bunch collard greens	10 minutes	½ cup
Kale	1 small bunch kale	10 minutes	½ cup
Swiss chard	1 small bunch Swiss chard	5 minutes	½ cup

1. Remove the leaves from the stalks, discarding the stalks, and wash the leaves extremely well (sand, grit, and insects often cling to leafy greens), swishing them in cold water and rinsing thoroughly. Chop the leaves roughly.

2. In a large sauté pan or skillet, heat 1 teaspoon olive oil over medium-high heat. Add the greens and sauté, stirring often, until the leaves become tender, about 5 minutes for chard, 10 minutes for kale and collard greens. Remove the pan from the heat and let the veggies cool, reserving any liquid in the pan.

3. When the greens have cooled, purée them in either a blender or food processor (or transfer to a bowl and purée using an immersion blender). For a thinner consistency, add some of the reserved cooking liquid or water.

STORAGE: Refrigerate leftover purée in an airtight container for up to 2 days or freeze for up to 3 months.

NOTES

Seven to Eight Months ● *Single-Ingredient Purées*

Quinoa and Banana Purée

SUPERFOOD GLUTEN-FREE NUT-FREE DAIRY-FREE VEGAN

MAKES 6 SERVINGS, ¼ CUP EACH
PREP TIME: 5 MINUTES • COOK TIME: 15 MINUTES

Not only is quinoa a superfood loaded with protein and fiber, but it also contains higher levels of essential amino acids than other cereals and gives fruit purées—in this case, banana—a delicious dose of texture. For babies eight months and up, try adding a little ground flax meal, which provides omega-3 fatty acids. This dish will likely become a morning staple in your house!

Tip: *Larger amounts of quinoa can be prepared in advance and stored in the refrigerator for up to 48 hours, then blended with banana or other soft fruits, or premade pureés. One benefit of quinoa is that it barely needs to be pureéd—the texture is already relatively smooth.*

1 cup water

½ cup quinoa

1 large banana, peeled

1. In a small pot with a lid, bring the water to a boil over medium heat.

2. Add the quinoa, cover the pot, reduce the heat to low, and simmer for about 15 minutes, or until the water has been absorbed. Allow to cool.

3. Slice the banana into 1-inch chunks.

4. In a blender or food processor, combine the cooled quinoa and banana, and purée until it reaches the desired consistency.

STORAGE: Leftover purée can be refrigerated in an airtight container for up to 2 days or frozen for up to 3 months.

NOTES

_____

_____

_____

Apple Pie Oatmeal Purée

NUT-FREE DAIRY-FREE VEGAN **GLUTEN-FREE**

MAKES 6 SERVINGS, ¼ CUP EACH
PREP TIME: 10 MINUTES • COOK TIME: 10 MINUTES

Filled with fiber, calcium, protein, and even some B vitamins, oats are a nutritious and delicious first food, especially when mixed with apples or other fruit. You and your baby will love the comforting, familiar scent that fills your kitchen while this is cooking.

Variation: *Cinnamon adds an authentic "pie" flavor to this recipe. While some parents are afraid to add herbs and spices to their baby's food, there's usually no reason for concern. Consult your pediatrician, and watch for reactions as you would with any other food. And if gluten is any concern for your family or your baby, make sure to buy oats labeled gluten-free to ensure there was no cross-contamination during processing.*

¼ cup steel-cut or old-fashioned oats

¾ cup water

1 large apple, peeled and cored

1. In a blender or food processor, grind the oats until they reach a powdery consistency.

2. Dice the apple into ½-inch cubes.

3. In a small pot with a lid, combine the apple, oats, and water and bring to a slow boil over medium heat. Cover and simmer, stirring frequently, until the apple is soft, about 10 minutes. Allow to cool.

4. If a smoother texture is desired, purée the mixture in a blender or food processor.

STORAGE: Leftover purée can be refrigerated in an airtight container for up to 2 days or frozen for up to 3 months.

NOTES

Avocado, Sweet Potato, and Brown Rice Purée

SUPERFOOD GLUTEN-FREE NUT-FREE DAIRY-FREE VEGAN

MAKES 6 SERVINGS, ¼ CUP EACH
PREP TIME: 5 MINUTES • COOK TIME: 8 MINUTES

Brown rice provides more fiber, protein, and B vitamins than white rice (which are stripped out during the refining process). Hearty and satisfying, with an interesting blend of textures, this wholesome meal will be just as appealing to older members of the family—before it goes in the blender, that is.

Tip: *Commercially prepared brown rice baby cereal can be used in place of cooked brown rice. Baby cereal is less flavorful and will give the mixture a smoother consistency.*

½ medium sweet potato, peeled

½ medium avocado, halved, pitted, and peeled

½ cup cooked brown rice

1. Cut the sweet potato into ½-inch dice.

2. Fill a medium saucepan with about 1 inch of water and bring to a simmer. Place the sweet potato in a steamer basket, set it over the simmering water, cover, and cook until tender, about 8 minutes. Allow to cool.

3. While the sweet potato is cooking, cut the avocado into 1-inch chunks.

4. In a blender or food processor, combine the avocado, cooled sweet potato, and rice, and purée until the mixture reaches the desired consistency.

STORAGE: Leftover purée can be refrigerated in an airtight container for up to 2 days.

NOTES

Blueberries and Quinoa Purée

SUPERFOOD **NUT-FREE** **DAIRY-FREE** **VEGAN**

MAKES 4 SERVINGS, ¼ CUP EACH
PREP TIME: 5 MINUTES • COOK TIME: 15 MINUTES

Mixing protein-packed quinoa with blueberries creates a delicious and nutritious treat for your baby. Blueberries add vitamin C, potassium, and fiber, making this cereal a yummy breakfast or super snack anytime of day.

¼ cup quinoa

1 cup water

¼ cup blueberries

1. In a blender or food processor, grind the quinoa until it reaches a powdery consistency.

2. In a saucepan, bring the water to a boil over high heat. Add the quinoa and simmer, whisking continuously, for 10 minutes.

3. Fill a medium saucepan with about 1 inch of water and bring to a simmer. Place the blueberries in a steamer basket, set it over the simmering water, cover, and cook until tender, about 5 minutes. Allow to cool.

4. In a blender or food processor, purée the cooled blueberries until smooth, adding water if necessary to achieve the desired consistency.

5. Stir the blueberry purée into the cereal.

STORAGE: Leftover purée can be refrigerated in an airtight container for up to 2 days or frozen for up to 3 months.

NOTES

Papaya, Kiwi, and Oatmeal Purée

SUPERFOOD   NUT-FREE   DAIRY-FREE   VEGAN   GLUTEN-FREE

MAKES 6 SERVINGS, ¼ CUP EACH
PREP TIME: 10 MINUTES • COOK TIME: 10 MINUTES

Originally known as Chinese gooseberry, kiwi is rich in vitamins A, C, and E; potassium; and folate, and it's high in fiber, too. Papaya, which contains beneficial digestive enzymes, can be helpful for babies with reflux and other tummy troubles.

Variation: *Nearly any fruit purée can be mixed with oatmeal to great success. Try bananas, apples, pears, peaches, plums, prunes, berries, or cantaloupe. If using bananas, peaches, apples, or pears, try adding a sprinkle of cinnamon (about ⅛ teaspoon).*

¼ cup steel-cut or old-fashioned oats

1 large kiwi, peeled

¾ cup water

¼ cup diced fresh papaya

1. In a blender or food processor, grind the oats until they reach a powdery consistency.

2. Cut the kiwi into 1-inch chunks.

3. In a saucepan, bring the water to a boil over high heat. Add the oats and simmer, whisking frequently, for 10 minutes.

4. In a blender or food processor, purée the papaya and kiwi until smooth (or slightly lumpy).

5. Stir the fruit purée into the cereal.

STORAGE: Leftover purée can be refrigerated in an airtight container for up to 2 days or frozen for up to 3 months.

NOTES

Blueberry-Apple Yogurt Purée

SUPERFOOD GLUTEN-FREE NUT-FREE VEGETARIAN

MAKES 6 SERVINGS, ¼ CUP EACH
PREP TIME: 5 MINUTES • COOK TIME: 12 MINUTES

As you've probably already discovered, cooked and puréed apples are a favorite first food with most babies. The addition of antioxidant-rich blueberries makes this classic even more nutritious and delicious. The blueberries cook along with the apples in this recipe, so don't worry too much about finding perfectly sweet berries. Just don't forget that bib—blueberry stains are very hard to wash out of clothes!

Variation: *If you'd like to make this dish when blueberries aren't in season, the same amount of frozen blueberries will work just as well as fresh; there's no need to thaw before cooking. Frozen blueberries will give this purée a richer, slightly sweeter flavor (think blueberry pie).*

3 medium apples, peeled and cored

½ cup blueberries

½ cup water

½ cup full-fat plain yogurt

1. Cut the apples into ½-inch cubes.

2. In a medium saucepan, combine the apples, blueberries, and water. Simmer over medium-low heat until the apples are tender and the blueberries burst, about 12 minutes. Remove from the heat and allow to cool. Do not drain.

3. Transfer the cooled fruit mixture, including any liquid in the pan, to a blender or food processor, and purée until it reaches the desired consistency.

4. Stir the puréed fruit mixture into the yogurt.

STORAGE: Leftover purée can be refrigerated in an airtight container for up to 3 days or frozen for up to 3 months.

NOTES

Kale and Avocado Purée

SUPERFOOD **GLUTEN-FREE** **NUT-FREE** **DAIRY-FREE** **VEGAN**

MAKES 6 SERVINGS, ¼ CUP EACH
PREP TIME: 5 MINUTES • COOK TIME: 8 MINUTES

Packed with calcium, folate, and antioxidants, kale is the king of leafy green vegetables and can be either sautéed or steamed before puréeing. When mixed with superfood avocado, it becomes a creamier, more kid-friendly dish. This basic mixture can serve as the base for a variety of combinations—try adding chicken, rice, quinoa, or bananas.

Warning: *Kale leaves are very thick and never break down into a perfectly smooth liquid. Expect any purée made with kale to be slightly speckled with emerald green flecks, but don't worry—these are easy for babies to chew and digest.*

2 cups torn fresh kale leaves

1 medium avocado, halved, pitted, and peeled

1. Fill a medium saucepan with about 1 inch of water and bring to a simmer. Place the kale in a steamer basket, set it over the simmering water, cover, and cook until tender, about 8 minutes. Allow to cool.

2. Cut the avocado into 1-inch chunks.

3. In a blender or food processor, purée the cooled kale and avocado until the mixture reaches the desired consistency. Add water if necessary.

STORAGE: Leftover purée can be refrigerated in an airtight container for up to 2 days.

NOTES

NEW FLAVORS AND TEXTURES

Peas, Pear, and Broccoli Purée

SUPERFOOD GLUTEN-FREE NUT-FREE DAIRY-FREE VEGAN

MAKES 3 SERVINGS, ¼ CUP EACH
PREP TIME: 5 MINUTES • COOK TIME: 10 MINUTES

Loaded with plenty of vitamin C and soluble fiber, broccoli makes a great addition to almost any baby food recipe—but its slightly bitter taste can be a tough sell for some little ones. Blending broccoli with mellow peas and mild pears is a gentle way to introduce your baby to this nutritional powerhouse. Also, be sure that the broccoli is steamed thoroughly, as this will remove some of its pungency.

Variation: *Swap out the pears for bananas if you want a thicker, creamier consistency. The sweetness of the bananas also helps mask the flavor of the broccoli more than the pears do, though it's a good idea to get babies used to the taste of green veggies as early as possible.*

1 large pear, peeled and cored

¼ cup broccoli florets

2 tablespoons fresh or frozen peas

1. Cut the pear into 1-inch chunks.

2. Fill a medium saucepan with about 1 inch of water and bring to a simmer. Place the pear and broccoli in a steamer basket, set it over the simmering water, cover, and cook for about 5 minutes.

3. Add the peas and steam for 5 minutes more. Allow to cool.

4. In a blender or food processor, purée the cooled pear, broccoli, and peas until the desired consistency is reached. Add water if necessary.

STORAGE: Leftover purée can be refrigerated in an airtight container for up to 2 days or frozen for up to 3 months.

NOTES _____

_____

_____

_____

Cauliflower and Sweet Potato Purée

GLUTEN-FREE **NUT-FREE** DAIRY-FREE VEGAN

MAKES 5 SERVINGS, ¼ CUP EACH
PREP TIME: 5 MINUTES • COOK TIME: 20 MINUTES

Like its cruciferous cousin broccoli, cauliflower contains phytochemicals (which are said to help prevent cancer) and lots of vitamin A. When steamed and puréed, cauliflower's light, creamy texture blends well with almost anything. Frozen cauliflower works well in this recipe, too. Slightly nutty in flavor, millet makes this a hearty meal perfect for winter nights.

Tip: *Cauliflower is also available in orange and even purple; these varieties offer intriguingly bright colors, and pretty much the same taste.*

1 medium sweet potato, peeled

1 cup cauliflower florets

¼ cup millet

½ cup water

1. Cut the sweet potato into ½-inch cubes.

2. Fill a medium saucepan with about 1 inch of water and bring to a simmer. Place the sweet potato and cauliflower in a steamer basket, set it over the simmering water, cover, and cook until tender, about 15 minutes.

3. Meanwhile, in a small saucepan with a lid, combine the millet and water, and bring to a boil over medium heat. Reduce the heat to low, cover the pot, and simmer until all the water has been absorbed, about 15 minutes. Stir occasionally.

4. Remove the millet from the heat and allow to cool, covered, for about 5 minutes.

5. In a blender or food processor, combine the sweet potato, cauliflower, and millet, and purée until the desired consistency is reached. Add water if necessary.

STORAGE: Leftover purée can be refrigerated in an airtight container for up to 3 days or frozen for up to 3 months.

NOTES

Kiwi, Asparagus, and Banana Purée

SUPERFOOD GLUTEN-FREE **NUT-FREE** DAIRY-FREE VEGAN

MAKES 5 SERVINGS, ¼ CUP EACH
PREP TIME: 5 MINUTES ● COOK TIME: 8 MINUTES

Asparagus is not only relatively high in protein for a vegetable (2 grams in just five spears), but also provides iron, fiber, folic acid, and even some calcium. When picking out asparagus, look for a bunch with stalks of uniform size and firm, not mushy, tips. While asparagus mixes well with many fruits, the smooth banana in this combo can help baby get used to the vegetable's sometimes slightly stringy texture.

Warning: *While kiwis are not highly allergenic, they are an acidic fruit, which may cause rashes around the mouth (or diaper area). If kiwi causes this type of reaction in your baby, try removing it from her diet for a week or two, then reintroducing it.*

1 cup trimmed asparagus spears

1 large banana, peeled

1 medium kiwi, peeled

1. Fill a medium saucepan with about 1 inch of water and bring to a simmer. Place the asparagus in a steamer basket, set it over the simmering water, cover, and cook until tender, about 8 minutes. Allow to cool.

2. Cut the kiwi and banana into 1-inch chunks.

3. In a blender or food processor, combine the cooled asparagus, kiwi, and banana, and purée until the desired consistency is reached. Add water if necessary.

   STORAGE: Leftover purée can be refrigerated in an airtight container for up to 2 days or frozen for up to 3 months.

   NOTES ————————————————————————

   ————————————————————————————————

   ————————————————————————————————

   ————————————————————————————————

Peach, Blueberries, and Carrot Purée

SUPERFOOD GLUTEN-FREE **NUT-FREE** DAIRY-FREE VEGAN

MAKES 6 SERVINGS, ¼ CUP EACH
PREP TIME: 5 MINUTES • COOK TIME: 8 MINUTES

Most babies love the mild, tangy sweetness of peaches, which are high in vitamins A and C, as well as fiber, and can help keep your baby regular. Blueberries add an intriguing texture to the mix, while the carrots bring a pleasant earthiness. Frozen blueberries or peaches can be used when fresh are out of season; you may need to steam these for a minute or two longer.

Tip: *Ripe peaches should be firm but slightly soft to the touch and very fragrant. Avoid peaches with bruises or flat areas, and watch out for wrinkly skin—this could be a sign that the peach was kept chilled after harvest for too long and became dehydrated.*

1 medium carrot, peeled

1 medium peach, pitted and peeled

¼ cup blueberries

1. Cut the carrot into ½-inch rounds.

2. Fill a medium saucepan with about 1 inch of water and bring to a simmer. Place the carrot in a steamer basket, set it over the simmering water, cover, and cook until tender, about 8 minutes. Allow to cool.

3. Cut the peach into 1-inch chunks.

4. In a blender or food processor, combine the cooled carrot, peaches, and blueberries, and purée until smooth. Add water if necessary to achieve the desired consistency.

STORAGE: Leftover purée can be refrigerated in an airtight container for up to 3 days or frozen for up to 3 months.

NOTES _____

_____

_____

Papaya, Banana, and Cantaloupe Yogurt

SUPERFOOD **GLUTEN-FREE** **NUT-FREE** **VEGETARIAN**

MAKES 4 SERVINGS, ¼ CUP EACH
PREP TIME: 10 MINUTES

Soothing and cool, cantaloupe is a refreshing warm-weather treat for all ages. Because you won't find canned or frozen versions in the grocery store, this is one fruit that can only be enjoyed fresh. It's high in vitamin A, beta-carotene, and calcium. In this dish, mixing cantaloupe with papaya and bananas gives the watery melon a creamier consistency. Choose cantaloupes with a light beige rind that are slightly soft on the "blossom" end.

Warning: *Because cantaloupes can sometimes carry salmonella on their rinds, it's important to handle and prepare the melon carefully. Make sure to purchase cantaloupe that isn't bruised or damaged, and refrigerate it promptly. Wash your hands with warm soapy water after handling, and scrub the entire melon with cool water and a produce brush immediately before cutting and eating.*

1 large banana, peeled

1 cup cantaloupe chunks

1 cup papaya chunks

¼ cup full-fat plain yogurt

1. Cut the banana into 1-inch chunks.

2. In a blender or food processor, combine the banana, cantaloupe, and papaya, and purée until smooth.

3. Stir the fruit purée into the yogurt.

STORAGE: Leftover purée can be refrigerated in an airtight container for up to 2 days.

NOTES

Broccoli, Cauliflower, and Carrot Purée

SUPERFOOD GLUTEN-FREE NUT-FREE DAIRY-FREE VEGAN

MAKES 4 SERVINGS, ¼ CUP EACH
PREP TIME: 5 MINUTES • COOK TIME: 12 MINUTES

There's a reason why these three veggies are traditionally presented as a side-dish medley. The sweet carrots and mild cauliflower nicely offset the sharper flavor of the broccoli, and the combination of nutrients can't be beat. This mix works especially well as a chunkier mash once your baby can tolerate thicker purées, as the broccoli and cauliflower give the carrots a more interesting texture.

Tip: *Use frozen broccoli, cauliflower, and/or carrots in place of fresh so you don't have to do any peeling or chopping. These three veggies are often sold in the same bag in the freezer section. If you do choose frozen, expect a more uniform texture and milder flavor; frozen broccoli also tends to steam more quickly than fresh.*

1 medium carrot, peeled   ½ cup cauliflower florets
½ cup broccoli florets

1. Cut the carrot into ½-inch slices.

2. Fill a medium saucepan with about 1 inch of water and bring to a simmer. Place the carrot, broccoli, and cauliflower in a steamer basket, set it over the simmering water, cover, and cook until tender, 10 to 12 minutes. Allow to cool.

3. In a blender or food processor, purée the cooled carrot, broccoli, and cauliflower until smooth. Add water if necessary to achieve the desired consistency.

STORAGE: Leftover purée can be refrigerated in an airtight container for up to 3 days or frozen for up to 3 months.

NOTES

Green Beans and Papaya Purée

GLUTEN-FREE **NUT-FREE** DAIRY-FREE VEGAN

MAKES 4 SERVINGS, ¼ CUP EACH
PREP TIME: 5 MINUTES • COOK TIME: 8 MINUTES

One of the milder-tasting vegetables, green beans are usually a favorite with babies, and they're bound to be an even bigger hit when mixed with delicate, velvety papaya. The fruit lends a welcome creaminess to the green beans, which can sometimes have a stringy texture when puréed. Try adding oatmeal or rice for a heartier meal.

Tip: *A papaya is fully ripe when it's bright yellow with smooth skin. Slightly green papayas can be ripened at home on your counter. When preparing a papaya, you can either scoop the flesh out using a melon baller or remove the skin using a vegetable peeler (papaya skins are relatively soft and thin) and then slice the fruit.*

1 cup trimmed fresh green beans   1 cup papaya chunks

1. Fill a medium saucepan with about 1 inch of water and bring to a simmer. Place the green beans in a steamer basket, set it over the simmering water, cover, and cook until tender, about 8 minutes. Allow to cool.

2. In a blender or food processor, purée the cooled green beans and the papaya until smooth. Add water if necessary to achieve the desired consistency.

   STORAGE: Leftover purée can be refrigerated in an airtight container for up to 2 days or frozen for up to 3 months.

   NOTES

Butternut Squash, Cauliflower, and Peas Purée

SUPERFOOD GLUTEN-FREE **NUT-FREE** DAIRY-FREE VEGAN

MAKES 4 SERVINGS, ¼ CUP EACH
PREP TIME: 5 MINUTES • COOK TIME: 15 MINUTES

It takes about 50 minutes to bake or roast butternut squash. Luckily, frozen butternut squash purée is just as nutritious as fresh and can be prepared in no time throughout the year. Its delicate, slightly nutty flavor complements almost any vegetable, fruit, or meat.

Variation: *Roasted butternut squash or baked sweet potatoes can be used in place of the frozen squash puree. Just add it to the blender with the peas and cauliflower. If using fresh vegetables, the purée can be frozen for up to 3 months.*

½ cup frozen cooked butternut
  squash purée

½ cup fresh or frozen peas
½ cup cauliflower florets

1. Prepare the butternut squash purée according to the package directions and place it in a medium bowl.

2. Fill a medium saucepan with about 1 inch of water and bring to a simmer. Place the peas in a steamer basket, set it over the simmering water, cover, and cook until tender, about 5 minutes. Allow to cool.

3. Remove the peas from the steamer basket and add the cauliflower. Cover and cook until tender, about 10 minutes. Allow to cool.

4. In a blender or food processor, purée the cooled cauliflower and peas until smooth. Add water if necessary to achieve the desired consistency.

5. Stir the cauliflower-pea purée into the butternut squash purée.

STORAGE: Leftover purée can be refrigerated in an airtight container for up to 3 days.

NOTES

Kiwi and Zucchini Purée

SUPERFOOD · GLUTEN-FREE · NUT-FREE · DAIRY-FREE · VEGAN

MAKES 3 SERVINGS, ¼ CUP EACH
PREP TIME: 5 MINUTES • COOK TIME: 8 MINUTES

This recipe doubles the green with a dynamic duo rich in vitamins A, C, and E. The bright, citrusy kiwi adds a zesty note to the mild, buttery zucchini, and babies love the almost jellylike texture these two foods have when combined. Try leaving the skin on the zucchini for babies eight months and older.

Tip: *Just in case you're wondering, there's no need to strain the black seeds out of your kiwi purée. They're perfectly edible! Another useful tip: You don't actually have to peel kiwi—you can simply cut it in half and scoop out the green insides.*

1 medium zucchini, peeled

1 medium kiwi, peeled

1. Cut the zucchini into 1-inch chunks.

2. Fill a medium saucepan with about 1 inch of water and bring to a simmer. Place the zucchini in a steamer basket, set it over the simmering water, cover, and cook until tender, about 8 minutes. Allow to cool.

3. While the zucchini is steaming, cut the kiwi into 1-inch slices.

4. In a blender or food processor, purée the cooled zucchini and kiwi until smooth. Add water if necessary to achieve the desired consistency.

STORAGE: Leftover purée can be refrigerated in an airtight container for up to 2 days or frozen for up to 3 months.

NOTES

Peach, Kale, and Tofu Purée

GLUTEN-FREE **NUT-FREE** DAIRY-FREE VEGAN

MAKES 4 SERVINGS, ¼ CUP EACH
PREP TIME: 5 MINUTES • COOK TIME: 5 MINUTES

Introducing baby to leafy greens as early as possible is a great idea, as they are the foundation for a healthy lifelong diet. Mixing these veggies with no-fail favorites like peaches is a clever way to get your baby used to their flavor while adding still more vitamins and minerals. For babies eight months and up, leave the skin on the peach for extra fiber.

Tip: *If your peach isn't especially ripe or sweet, toss it in the steamer basket with the kale—but only for about 5 minutes. Cooking fruit, even for a short period of time, helps draw out the fruit's natural sugars; cooking it for too long will begin to destroy the nutrients it contains.*

2 cups torn fresh kale leaves

1 medium peach, pitted and peeled

¼ cup diced firm tofu

1. Fill a medium saucepan with about 1 inch of water and bring to a simmer. Place the kale in a steamer basket, set it over the simmering water, cover, and cook until tender, about 5 minutes. Allow to cool.

2. Slice the peach into 1-inch chunks.

3. In a blender or food processor, purée the cooled kale, peach, and tofu until the mixture reaches the desired consistency. Add water if necessary.

STORAGE: Leftover purée can be refrigerated in an airtight container for up to 2 days or frozen for up to 3 months.

NOTES

Watermelon and Pear Purée

MAKES 8 SERVINGS, ¼ CUP EACH
PREP TIME: 5 MINUTES • COOK TIME: 8 MINUTES

More than just a standard dessert at barbecues and picnics, watermelon is actually an extremely nutritious treat: High in lycopene (an antioxidant linked to cancer prevention) and arginine (thought to promote heart health), it's also packed with vitamins A and C and is rich in electrolytes, which will do a better job of keeping baby hydrated than any artificially flavored sports drink ever could!

Tip: *Contrary to popular belief, "tapping" a watermelon to see if it's ripe isn't the best method. Instead, look for watermelons that have dark green rinds free of cuts and bruises and have a creamy yellow spot on the bottom. They should also be relatively heavy for their size. Store in a cool, well-ventilated place; once cut, keep in the refrigerator.*

1 large pear, cored and peeled   1 cup seedless watermelon chunks

1. Cut the pear into 1-inch chunks.

2. Fill a medium saucepan with about 1 inch of water and bring to a simmer. Place the pear in a steamer basket, set it over the simmering water, cover, and cook until tender, about 8 minutes. Allow to cool.

3. In a blender or food processor, purée the cooled pear and watermelon until the mixture reaches the desired consistency. Add water if necessary.

STORAGE: Leftover purée can be refrigerated in an airtight container for up to 2 days or frozen for up to 3 months.

NOTES

Asparagus, Honeydew, and Peas Purée

GLUTEN-FREE | NUT-FREE | DAIRY-FREE | VEGAN

MAKES 5 SERVINGS, ¼ CUP EACH
PREP TIME: 5 MINUTES • COOK TIME: 10 MINUTES

Low in calories and high in vitamins A and C, honeydew has a distinctive taste and juicy texture loved by kids of all ages. In this recipe, the almost flowery flavor of the melon brings out the just-picked taste of fresh asparagus spears and sweet green peas; the watery consistency also gives the starchier peas a pleasant lift.

Tip: *When choosing honeydew, look for a waxy (not fuzzy) rind that springs back when pressed. Avoid rinds with cuts, cracks, dry areas, or soft spots larger than 2 inches across. The melon should also feel heavy for its size.*

1 cup trimmed asparagus spears   ½ cup honeydew chunks
½ cup fresh or frozen peas

1. Fill a medium saucepan with about 1 inch of water and bring to a simmer. Place the asparagus in a steamer basket, set it over the simmering water, cover, and cook for about 5 minutes.

2. Add the peas to the steamer basket, cover, and cook for about 5 minutes more. Allow to cool.

3. In a blender or food processor, purée the cooled asparagus and peas and the honeydew until the desired consistency is reached. Add water if necessary.

STORAGE: Leftover purée can be refrigerated in an airtight container for up to 2 days or frozen for up to 3 months.

NOTES ———————————————————————————

———————————————————————————————

———————————————————————————————

———————————————————————————————

Apricot, Cherries, and Banana Purée

SUPERFOOD GLUTEN-FREE **NUT-FREE** DAIRY-FREE VEGAN

MAKES 4 SERVINGS, ¼ CUP EACH
PREP TIME: 5 MINUTES • COOK TIME: 5 MINUTES

One of the most eagerly anticipated treats of the summer, cherries are more than just delicious. They're also surprisingly high in calcium as well as vitamins A and C. If cherries are ripe and sweet enough, there's no need to steam them; if not, steaming for just a few minutes can help bring out their flavor. The same goes for the apricots in this recipe. And don't worry about peeling the cherries; the skins will purée easily.

Tip: *Ripe apricots should be firm but slightly soft to the touch and vivid orange in hue. When choosing cherries, look for a deep saturation of color and firm skins.*

1 medium apricot, pitted

1 large banana, peeled

½ cup cherries, pitted and halved

1. Cut the apricot into 1-inch chunks.

2. Fill a medium saucepan with about 1 inch of water and bring to a simmer. Place the cherries and apricot in a steamer basket, set it over the simmering water, cover, and cook until tender, about 5 minutes. Allow to cool.

3. Cut the banana into 1-inch slices.

4. In a blender or food processor, purée the cooled cherries and apricot and the banana until smooth. Add water if necessary to achieve the desired consistency.

STORAGE: Leftover purée can be refrigerated in an airtight container for up to 3 days or frozen for up to 3 months.

NOTES

Chicken, Pears, and Quinoa Purée

NUT-FREE GLUTEN-FREE DAIRY-FREE

MAKES 4 SERVINGS, ¼ CUP EACH
PREP TIME: 5 MINUTES • COOK TIME: 8 MINUTES

Two mild foods that taste great together, chicken and pears provide baby with a solid serving of protein, vitamin C, fiber, magnesium, and selenium. If your chicken happens to be a bit on the dry side, don't worry—the refreshing pear purée will add just enough moisture to make this dish go down easy! Quinoa adds protein and fiber, and some texture depending upon how smoothly it's pureed.

Variation: *Apples can be substituted for pears in this recipe; use one large apple, cored, peeled, and steamed in the same way. Try Golden Delicious if available. One of the sweetest, most mellow varieties of apple, it works better with chicken than Granny Smith or McIntosh, for example, which are more tart.*

1 large pear, cored and peeled

½ cup diced cooked chicken breast

½ cup cooked quinoa (see page 35)

1. Cut the pear into 1-inch chunks.

2. Fill a medium saucepan with about 1 inch of water and bring to a simmer. Place the pears in a steamer basket, set it over the simmering water, cover, and cook until tender, about 8 minutes. Allow to cool.

3. In a blender or food processor, purée the cooled pears, chicken, and quinoa until the desired consistency is reached. Add water if necessary.

STORAGE: Leftover purée can be refrigerated in an airtight container for up to 3 days or frozen for up to 3 months.

NOTES

Chicken and Avocado Purée

NUT-FREE GLUTEN-FREE DAIRY-FREE

MAKES 6 SERVINGS, ¼ CUP EACH
PREP TIME: 5 MINUTES

If you've ever eaten chicken enchiladas with guacamole or a grilled chicken breast sandwich topped with avocado, you know exactly how scrumptious the combination in this recipe can be—and the flavors work just as well together in purée form. In fact, you might be tempted to dip a tortilla chip in the leftovers!

Variation: *The creamy texture of avocado mixes just as well with turkey or beef as it does with chicken. Combining beef and avocado will result in a Mexican "seven-layer dip" sort of flavor, while adding avocado to turkey can help offset the sometimes dry consistency of the white meat.*

1 medium avocado, halved, pitted, and peeled

½ cup diced cooked chicken breast

1. Cut the avocado into 1-inch chunks.

2. In a blender or food processor, purée the avocado and chicken until the desired consistency is reached. Add water if necessary.

STORAGE: Leftover purée can be refrigerated in an airtight container for up to 2 days.

NOTES

Chicken, Apricots, and Prunes Purée

NUT-FREE GLUTEN-FREE DAIRY-FREE

MAKES 6 SERVINGS, ¼ CUP EACH
PREP TIME: 5 MINUTES • COOK TIME: 5 MINUTES

While many people are tempted to overlook fresh apricots because they can sometimes be mealy and dry, these little fruits pack a big nutritional punch—and when picked properly, they're quite a treat! Perfect in chutneys and jam, apricots make a suitable companion to the chicken in this recipe, as neither taste overwhelms the other. No need to peel the apricots; steaming will make their skins soft.

Variation: *If you can't find fresh, ripe apricots at the store, consider using dried instead—dried apricots are always sweet! Stick to unsulphured varieties, and purée the same way you would prunes.*

1 medium apricot, pitted

½ cup diced cooked chicken breast

¼ cup prune purée (see page 31)

1. Cut the apricot into 1-inch chunks.

2. Fill a medium saucepan with about 1 inch of water and bring to a simmer. Place the apricot in a steamer basket, set it over the simmering water, cover, and cook until tender, about 5 minutes. Allow to cool.

3. In a blender or food processor, purée the cooled apricot and chicken until the desired consistency is reached. Add water if necessary, and mix with prune purée.

STORAGE: Leftover purée can be refrigerated in an airtight container for up to 3 days or frozen for up to 3 months.

NOTES

Chicken and Zucchini Purée

NUT-FREE GLUTEN-FREE DAIRY-FREE

MAKES 6 SERVINGS, ¼ CUP EACH
PREP TIME: 5 MINUTES • COOK TIME: 5 MINUTES

Mellow and almost buttery in flavor, zucchini tends to pick up the flavor of whatever it's paired with. In this recipe, the summer squash adds a creamy sweetness to the savory chicken; its high water content will also keep the purée from getting too mealy. If your baby's digestive system can tolerate the extra fiber, leave the skin on the zucchini—just be sure to wash it well.

Tip: *Like parsnips, sweet potatoes, butternut squash, and even asparagus, zucchini develops a deeper, more complex flavor when roasted. To use roasted zucchini instead of steamed in this recipe, preheat the oven to 400°F. Chop the zucchini into ¼-inch cubes and toss them with 1 teaspoon of olive oil in a medium bowl. Spread the zucchini cubes in a single layer on a 9-by-13-inch baking pan, leaving about 1 inch of space between them. Bake for 15 to 20 minutes, or until tender.*

1 medium zucchini, peeled   ½ cup diced cooked chicken breast

1. Cut the zucchini into 1-inch chunks.

2. Fill a medium saucepan with about 1 inch of water and bring to a simmer. Place the zucchini in a steamer basket, set it over the simmering water, cover, and cook until tender, about 5 minutes. Allow to cool.

3. In a blender or food processor, purée the zucchini and chicken until the desired consistency is reached. Add water if necessary.

STORAGE: Leftover purée can be refrigerated in an airtight container for up to 3 days or frozen for up to 3 months.

NOTES _____

_____

_____

_____

Turkey, Mango, and Cucumber Purée

DAIRY-FREE **GLUTEN-FREE** **NUT-FREE**

MAKES 4 SERVINGS, ¼ CUP EACH

PREP TIME: 5 MINUTES • COOK TIME: 15 MINUTES

Give turkey a tropical twist with the addition of ripe, juicy mango, which is high in anti-oxidants, beta-carotene, and vitamin K. Fun fact: Mangos are part of the drupe family, a type of fruit in which an outer fleshy part surrounds a pit; olives, coconuts, and dates are also drupes.

Variation: *If you find that ground turkey is too dry, try using a mixture of half turkey and half ground beef. Some people who are trying to eat less red meat find this makes the transition from beef to turkey easier. Though your baby likely won't know the difference, he may appreciate the more succulent texture!*

1 teaspoon olive oil

½ pound ground turkey

½ cup cubed mango (see page 32)

½ cup cucumber, peeled and cubed

1. In a medium sauté pan or skillet, heat the olive oil over medium heat.

2. Add the ground turkey and reduce the heat to medium-low. Cook, stirring frequently and breaking up the turkey into small pieces with a spoon as it browns, for about 15 minutes, until browned evenly and cooked through.

3. Drain the excess fat from the pan and allow the turkey to cool.

4. In a blender or food processor, combine the cooled turkey, mango, and cucumber, and purée until the desired consistency is reached. Add water if necessary.

STORAGE: Leftover purée can be refrigerated in an airtight container for up to 3 days or frozen for up to 3 months.

NOTES

Turkey and Plums Purée

MAKES 4 SERVINGS, ¼ CUP EACH
PREP TIME: 5 MINUTES ● COOK TIME: 15 MINUTES

Did you know there are nearly 40 different types of plums? The stone fruit comes in colors from black to red to green to yellow, though you'll probably find only a few of these shades at your local grocery store—the most common varieties are black and red. While some plums are sweeter than others, they're all high in vitamin C, calcium, and fiber.

Tip: *If you're stuck with a plum that's not particularly sweet, steam the fruit for about 5 minutes before puréeing it with the turkey. This will help bring out the plum's natural sugars. Steaming will make the plum softer, too.*

1 teaspoon olive oil

½ pound ground turkey

1 large plum, pitted and peeled

1. In a medium sauté pan or skillet, heat the olive oil over medium heat.

2. Add the ground turkey and reduce the heat to medium-low. Cook, stirring frequently and breaking up the turkey into small pieces with a spoon as it browns, for about 15 minutes, until browned evenly and cooked through.

3. While the turkey is cooking, cut the plum into ½-inch chunks.

4. Drain the excess fat from the pan with the turkey and allow the turkey to cool.

5. In a blender or food processor, purée the cooled turkey and plum until the desired consistency is reached. Add water if necessary.

STORAGE: Leftover purée can be refrigerated in an airtight container for up to 3 days or frozen for up to 3 months.

NOTES

Turkey, Carrots, and Broccoli Purée

DAIRY-FREE · GLUTEN-FREE · NUT-FREE

MAKES 4 SERVINGS, ¼ CUP EACH
PREP TIME: 5 MINUTES • COOK TIME: 15 MINUTES

Someday, you'll pack a turkey sandwich with carrot sticks in your little one's lunchbox. For now, you can give him the same nutritious meal on a spoon (with the sneaky addition of super-nutritious broccoli!).

Variation: *Try mixing turkey with other steamed or roasted veggies, such as sweet potatoes or butternut squash.*

1 large carrot, peeled
½ cup broccoli florets

1 teaspoon olive oil
½ pound ground turkey

1. Cut the carrot into ½-inch slices.

2. Fill a medium saucepan with about 1 inch of water and bring to a simmer. Place the carrots and broccoli in a steamer basket, set it over the simmering water, cover, and cook until tender when pierced with a fork or knife, 8 to 10 minutes. Allow to cool.

3. While the carrots and broccoli are steaming, heat the olive oil over medium heat in a medium sauté pan or skillet.

4. Add the ground turkey and reduce the heat to medium-low. Cook, stirring frequently and breaking up the turkey into small pieces with a spoon as it browns, for about 15 minutes, until browned evenly and cooked through.

5. Drain the excess fat from the pan and allow the turkey to cool.

6. In a blender or food processor, purée the cooled turkey, carrots, and broccoli until the desired consistency is reached. Add water if necessary.

STORAGE: Leftover purée can be refrigerated in an airtight container for up to 3 days or frozen for up to 3 months.

NOTES

Pork and Apples Purée

NUT-FREE GLUTEN-FREE DAIRY-FREE

MAKES 4 SERVINGS, ¼ CUP EACH

PREP TIME: 5 MINUTES • COOK TIME: 5 MINUTES

There's a reason why pairing pork chops and applesauce has become a time-honored tradition: the combination is delicious! Of course, there's no reason to stick to chops when it comes to re-creating this meal for your baby. In fact, we recommend using cooked pork loin, which is lean but tends to be juicier than chops. Packed with protein and higher in B vitamins than any other type of meat, pork's mild flavor makes it a versatile addition to many baby purées and mashes.

Tip: *When looking for pork, try to stick with free-range and/or antibiotic-free varieties, just as you would with beef or chicken. And make sure your pork is cooked thoroughly, to at least 145°F, the USDA's recommended internal temperature for pork.*

1 large apple, cored and peeled   ½ cup diced, cooked pork loin

1. Cut the apple into 1-inch chunks.

2. Fill a medium saucepan with about 1 inch of water and bring to a simmer. Place the apple in a steamer basket, set it over the simmering water, cover, and cook until tender, about 5 minutes. Allow to cool.

3. In a blender or food processor, purée the cooled apple and pork until the desired consistency is reached. Add water if necessary.

STORAGE: Leftover purée can be refrigerated in an airtight container for up to 3 days or frozen for up to 3 months.

NOTES ————————————————————————

———————————————————————————————————

———————————————————————————————————

———————————————————————————————————

Pork, Carrots, and Brown Rice Purée

SUPERFOOD **DAIRY-FREE** **GLUTEN-FREE** **NUT-FREE**

MAKES 6 SERVINGS, ¼ CUP EACH
PREP TIME: 5 MINUTES • COOK TIME: 10 MINUTES

A perfect recipe for using up dinnertime leftovers, this combination of mellow tastes makes for a yummy meal. Fresh carrots bring out the pork's natural sweetness, while aromatic brown rice rounds out the flavors nicely. For added color and texture, toss in some fresh steamed peas.

Variation: *Instead of steaming carrots for this recipe, try roasting a larger batch when you prepare the pork loin and rice (which the whole family can enjoy). Preheat the oven to 400°F. Chop 4 peeled carrots into ¼-inch chunks and place them in a medium bowl. Toss with 1 teaspoon olive oil. Spread the carrots out in a single layer on a baking pan. Bake for 25 minutes, or until the carrots are tender.*

1 large carrot, peeled   ½ cup cooked brown rice (see page 35)
½ cup diced cooked pork loin

1. Cut the carrot into ½-inch slices.

2. Fill a medium saucepan with about 1 inch of water and bring to a simmer. Place the carrot in a steamer basket, set it over the simmering water, cover, and cook until tender when pierced with a fork or knife, 8 to 10 minutes. Allow to cool.

3. In a blender or food processor, combine the cooled carrot, pork, and rice and purée until the desired consistency is reached. Add water if necessary.

STORAGE: Leftover purée can be refrigerated in an airtight container for up to 3 days or frozen for up to 3 months.

NOTES _____

_____

_____

Beef, Sweet Potatoes, and Swiss Chard Purée

DAIRY-FREE **NUT-FREE** GLUTEN-FREE

MAKES 6 SERVINGS, ¼ CUP EACH
PREP TIME: 5 MINUTES • COOK TIME: 20 MINUTES

Creamy, starchy sweet potatoes add to the richness of the beef and help soak up the juices—think of a yummy pot roast surrounded by roasted root veggies with a side of delicious, iron-rich greens. Packed with protein, fiber, and vitamins A and B, this meal is as nourishing as it is delectable.

1 medium sweet potato, peeled

½ cup chopped Swiss chard leaves

½ pound ground beef

1. Cut the sweet potato into ½-inch cubes.

2. Fill a medium saucepan with about 1 inch of water and bring to a simmer. Place the sweet potatoes and chard in a steamer basket, set it over the simmering water, cover, and cook until tender, about 15 minutes. Allow to cool.

3. While the sweet potatoes and chard are steaming, cook the ground beef over medium-low heat in a medium frying pan, stirring frequently and breaking the beef into small pieces with a spoon as it browns, for about 15 minutes, until browned evenly and cooked through.

4. Drain the excess fat from the pan and allow the beef to cool.

5. In a blender or food processor, purée the cooled beef, sweet potatoes, and chard until the desired consistency is reached. Add water if necessary.

STORAGE: Leftover purée can be refrigerated in an airtight container for up to 3 days or frozen for up to 3 months.

NOTES

Beef and Parsnips Purée

DAIRY-FREE **NUT-FREE** **GLUTEN-FREE**

MAKES 4 SERVINGS, ¼ CUP EACH
PREP TIME: 5 MINUTES • COOK TIME: 15 MINUTES

Parsnips look like a white version of carrots, but they have a taste all their own: sweet, slightly nutty, and completely delicious. They also contain potassium, fiber, and B vitamins. Look for parsnips that are pale in color and firm.

Tip: *If you have time, roast the parsnips before puréeing for wonderful flavor. Preheat the oven to 400°F. Chop the parsnip into ¼-inch cubes, and toss with 1 teaspoon olive oil in a medium bowl. Spread them out in a single layer on a baking pan and bake for 35 to 40 minutes, or until the parsnips are tender.*

1 medium parsnip, peeled   ½ pound ground beef

1. Cut the parsnip into ½-inch chunks.

2. Fill a medium saucepan with about 1 inch of water and bring to a simmer. Place the parsnip in a steamer basket, set it over the simmering water, cover, and cook until tender, 8 to 10 minutes. Allow to cool.

3. While the parsnip is steaming, cook the ground beef over medium-low heat in a medium sauté pan or skillet, stirring frequently and breaking the beef into small pieces with a spoon as it browns, for about 15 minutes, until browned evenly and cooked through.

4. Drain the excess fat from the pan, and allow the beef to cool.

5. In a blender or food processor, purée the cooled beef and parsnips until the desired consistency is reached. Add water if necessary.

STORAGE: Leftover purée can be refrigerated in an airtight container for up to 3 days or frozen for up to 3 months.

NOTES ————————————————————————————————

Beef and Green Beans Purée

DAIRY-FREE **NUT-FREE** **GLUTEN-FREE**

MAKES 4 SERVINGS, ¼ CUP EACH
PREP TIME: 5 MINUTES • COOK TIME: 15 MINUTES

While green beans in jarred baby food tend to be somewhat bitter, the beans in this homemade blend retain their just-picked sweetness. The beef is juicy and flavorful, not gelatinous and bland, as is the case with some commercial baby foods.

Variation: *If you're using frozen green beans, why not try frozen mixed veggies instead, for a stewlike purée? Simply substitute the same amount of frozen green beans, carrots, and peas (or whatever veggies you want to experiment with) for the fresh beans.*

½ cup trimmed green beans   ½ pound ground beef

1. Fill a medium saucepan with about 1 inch of water and bring to a simmer. Place the green beans in a steamer basket, set it over the simmering water, cover, and cook until tender when pierced with a fork or knife, about 5 minutes. Allow to cool.

2. While the green beans are steaming, cook the ground beef over medium-low heat in a medium sauté pan or skillet, stirring frequently and breaking the beef into small pieces with a spoon as it browns, for about 15 minutes, until browned evenly and cooked through.

3. Drain the excess fat from the pan and allow the beef to cool.

4. In a blender or food processor, purée the cooled beef and green beans until the desired consistency is reached. Add water if necessary.

STORAGE: Leftover purée can be refrigerated in an airtight container for up to 3 days or frozen for up to 3 months.

NOTES

Balanced Bites and Finger Foods

Chances are you're spending most of your time just trying to keep up with your little one these days. He's most likely crawling (possibly at quite a fast pace) and cruising around the house while holding on to furniture—he might even be walking on his own! He's probably mastered the art of sitting up for long periods of time unassisted, and you'll notice that he's starting to understand language, responding to certain words and maybe shaking his head to indicate "no" or "yes." Plus, the pincer grasp (using his thumb and forefinger to pick up objects) he's been developing over the past few months is just about perfected at this point, which makes this a good time to tackle the skill of self-feeding.

IS BABY READY?

In general, babies aren't very subtle when it comes to letting you know they're ready for a more independent approach to mealtime—by the age of nine months, your child will most likely be grabbing for the spoon as you're trying to feed her or even attempting to steal dinner from your plate!

Baby's first finger foods don't have to be complicated—in fact, the simpler to prepare, the better, especially considering not all of these morsels are going to make it into her mouth. Stick to soft foods—as your little one probably doesn't have too many teeth to work with just yet—with as much nutrition as possible packed into every bite.

Introduce finger foods slowly, serving no more than four or five pieces at a time, and monitor your baby carefully while she eats. Don't worry if more food ends up on the floor than in her mouth at first. Learning to self-feed is all about experimentation, so it's perfectly normal for your baby to "play" with her food at this point.

In addition to providing recipes for simple finger foods, this chapter also includes recipes for meals that look more like what you're eating. With their introduction here, they're categorized as baby meals. With a few modifications, you might find that the recipes in this section work as family meals, not just baby meals.

RECOMMENDED SERVING SIZES

Between nine and eleven months of age, your baby should gradually move up to three solid meals a day, with each meal consisting of one to three servings of combinations of the food groups below. Servings should still be about the size of your baby's fist, including:

- ¼ to ½ cup fruit

- ¼ to ½ cup vegetables

- ⅛ to ¼ cup protein-rich foods

- ⅓ cup dairy (or ½ ounce cheese)

- ¼ to ½ cup cereal

BREAST MILK OR FORMULA

Now that your baby is eating solid foods more regularly, you may be tempted to cut back on breastfeeding or bottle feeding—but don't rush it. Through about his first birthday, he'll still need 24 to 32 ounces of breast milk or formula in every 24-hour period.

DEALING WITH A PICKY EATER

If your baby turns up his nose at all of your carefully prepared purées and consistently hides his finger foods in the seat of his high chair, don't despair. When it comes to feeding babies and toddlers, the best-laid meals often go to waste. Some kids seem fussy about food because they have especially sensitive taste buds; others are just naturally more cautious when it comes to trying new things. As long as your pediatrician says weight gain and growth are normal, there's most likely no reason to worry. And while you should never force your baby to eat a certain food, there are some tips that can help make the transition to solids easier:

- Keep distractions to a minimum during mealtime by turning off the TV and keeping toys and books away from his high chair tray.

- Experiment with different textures and temperatures. Some babies like it hot (but not too hot!); others prefer cool or room-temperature foods. Some babies like slippery, wet meals on a spoon; others like firm chunks they can feed themselves.

- Make sure your baby isn't too full of breast milk or formula when he sits down to eat. Try nursing or giving a bottle after mealtime.

NEW FOODS TO INTRODUCE

At nine months:

Beans	Cottage cheese	Onions	Turnips
Cheese	Cream cheese	Peppers	Wheat
Chickpeas	Lentils	Potatoes (white)	

At ten months:

Corn	Fish	Strawberries

Peach, Plum, and Strawberry Oatmeal Purée

DAIRY-FREE **NUT-FREE** **GLUTEN-FREE**

MAKES 6 SERVINGS, ¼ CUP EACH
PREP TIME: 5 MINUTES • COOK TIME: 10 MINUTES

Old-fashioned rolled oats cook in nearly half the time as steel cut, and are virtually identical nutritionally. If you're looking to spend even less time in the kitchen, try "quick rolled oats," which cook in about 1 minute.

Variation: *Skip the sweetened packets of instant "peaches and cream" or "strawberries and cream" oatmeal, and make your own version by omitting the plum and adding ½ cup full-fat plain yogurt and ½ teaspoon cinnamon to the cereal after puréeing.*

1 cup water

½ cup old-fashioned rolled oats

1 medium peach, pitted and peeled

1 medium plum, pitted and peeled

¼ cup sliced strawberries

1. In a small saucepan with a lid, bring the water to a boil over high heat.

2. Reduce the heat to low and stir in the oats. Simmer, uncovered, stirring occasionally, for about 10 minutes, until the liquid has been absorbed (the oats shouldn't be too dry, however). Remove the pan from the heat and allow the oats to cool.

3. Cut the peach and plum into ½-inch chunks.

4. Place the peach, plum, strawberries, and cooled oats in a blender or food processor and purée until smooth (or slightly lumpy).

STORAGE: Leftover purée can be refrigerated in an airtight container for up to 2 days or frozen for up to 3 months.

NOTES

Chickpea, Sweet Potato, and Cauliflower Purée

DAIRY-FREE GLUTEN-FREE **NUT-FREE** VEGAN

MAKES 5 SERVINGS, ¼ CUP EACH
PREP TIME: 5 MINUTES • COOK TIME: 15 MINUTES

A staple in vegetarian diets across the globe, chickpeas are high in fiber, protein, zinc, manganese, folate, and even iron! While these nifty little legumes have been known to cause gas in babies, this can be avoided by rinsing canned chickpeas before using them (or soaking dried chickpeas before cooking). The chickpeas in this recipe lend a much-needed savory note to the sweet potatoes and cauliflower.

Tip: *Try adding chickpeas to a variety of other purées, too. Not only will the chickpeas give your baby much-needed protein, they'll help keep certain fruit and vegetable purées from becoming too runny (particularly those featuring watery items such as zucchini).*

1 medium sweet potato, peeled

1 cup cauliflower florets

¼ cup canned chickpeas, drained and rinsed

1. Cut the sweet potato into ½-inch cubes.

2. Fill a medium saucepan with about 1 inch of water and bring to a simmer. Place the sweet potato and cauliflower in a steamer basket, set it over the simmering water, cover, and cook until tender, about 15 minutes. Allow to cool.

3. In a blender or food processor, purée the cooled sweet potato and cauliflower and the chickpeas until the desired consistency is reached. Add water if necessary.

STORAGE: Leftover purée can be refrigerated in an airtight container for up to 3 days or frozen for up to 3 months.

NOTES

Black Beans, Collard Greens, and Parsnip Purée

DAIRY-FREE GLUTEN-FREE **NUT-FREE** VEGAN

MAKES 5 SERVINGS, ¼ CUP EACH
PREP TIME: 5 MINUTES • COOK TIME: 10 MINUTES

Inexpensive, flavorful, and a fabulous source of protein, black beans result in softer and smoother purées than some other varieties of beans. The sweetness of the parsnips off-sets the slightly bitter quality of the collard greens, while all three ingredients combined provide an interesting array of textures.

Tip: *When shopping for collards, always look for vivid, deep green leaves. Smaller leaves will be sweeter and more tender than larger leaves. Store collards, bagged, in the refrigerator for 3 to 5 days.*

1 medium parsnip, peeled

1 cup chopped collard green leaves

¼ cup rinsed canned black beans, drained and rinsed

1. Cut the parsnip into ½-inch rounds.

2. Fill a medium saucepan with about 1 inch of water and bring to a simmer. Place the parsnip and collard greens in a steamer basket, set it over the simmering water, cover, and cook for about 5 minutes. Remove the greens and steam until the parsnip is tender, about 5 minutes more. Allow both vegetables to cool.

3. In a blender or food processor, purée the cooled collard greens and parsnip and the black beans until the desired consistency is reached. Add water if necessary.

STORAGE: Leftover purée can be refrigerated in an airtight container for up to 3 days or frozen for up to 3 months.

NOTES

Chicken, Apple, and Sweet Potato Purée

DAIRY-FREE **NUT-FREE** **GLUTEN-FREE**

MAKES 6 SERVINGS, ¼ CUP EACH
PREP TIME: 5 MINUTES • COOK TIME: 10 MINUTES

High in protein and iron, chicken is one of the most easily digestible meats. When first introducing your baby to chicken, try pairing the meat with sweet fruits and veggies like apples and sweet potatoes. This combination provides a tasty balance of fiber, vitamins, and minerals, and works as either a smooth or chunky purée.

1 large apple, cored and peeled

1 medium sweet potato, peeled

½ cup diced cooked chicken breast

1. Cut the apple and sweet potato into ½-inch cubes.

2. Fill a medium saucepan with about 1 inch of water, and bring to a simmer. Place the sweet potato in a steamer basket, set it over the simmering water, cover, and cook for about 5 minutes.

3. Add the apple and steam for 5 minutes more, or until both are tender. Allow to cool.

4. In a blender or food processor, purée the cooled sweet potato and apple and the chicken until the desired consistency is reached. Add water if necessary.

STORAGE: Leftover purée can be refrigerated in an airtight container for up to 3 days or frozen for up to 3 months.

NOTES

Chicken, Peas, and Banana Purée

SUPERFOOD **DAIRY-FREE** **NUT-FREE** **GLUTEN-FREE**

MAKES 4 SERVINGS, ¼ CUP EACH
PREP TIME: 5 MINUTES • COOK TIME: 5 MINUTES

Perfect for any baby with a sweet tooth—which means just about every baby—this recipe blends the mildest of all meats, veggies, and fruits into one mega-mellow mash. When baby is ready to try feeding himself, try serving a few bites of each of these foods on his high chair tray without puréeing; they all make great first finger foods.

Variation: *Thanks to the creamy sweetness of the bananas, you can easily replace the peas in this recipe with a more bitter-tasting green veggie such as kale, collard greens, or Swiss chard. Any of these will give the purée a thinner, grittier consistency.*

½ cup fresh or frozen peas

1 large banana, peeled

½ cup diced cooked chicken breast

1. Fill a medium saucepan with about 1 inch of water and bring to a simmer. Place the peas in a steamer basket, set it over the simmering water, cover, and cook until tender, about 5 minutes. Allow to cool.

2. Cut the banana into 1-inch chunks.

3. In a blender or food processor, purée the cooled peas, banana, and chicken until the desired consistency is reached. Add water if necessary.

STORAGE: Leftover purée can be refrigerated in an airtight container for up to 3 days or frozen for up to 3 months.

NOTES _____

_____

_____

_____

Chicken, Peach, and Pumpkin Purée

DAIRY-FREE **NUT-FREE** GLUTEN-FREE

MAKES 4 SERVINGS, ¼ CUP EACH

PREP TIME: 5 MINUTES ● COOK TIME: 5 MINUTES

Pumpkins aren't just for holiday pies and jack-o'-lanterns. They're actually extremely nutritious, boasting plenty of vitamin A, beta-carotene, potassium, and even iron and protein. Cooking pumpkin from scratch can be time-consuming—and pumpkin season is brief—but canned purées are just as beneficial and tasty. Make sure to buy pure pumpkin purée instead of pumpkin pie filling, which has added sweeteners and flavorings. Try using any leftover canned purée in pancakes.

Variation: *As with peach cobbler or pumpkin pie, a dash of cinnamon complements this dish nicely. Cinnamon is also a common ingredient in Greek and Moroccan chicken dishes. Try the combination in grown-up meals, too!*

1 medium peach, pitted

½ cup canned pure pumpkin purée

½ cup diced cooked chicken breast

1. Peel the peach, if baby can't tolerate the skin, and cut the flesh into 1-inch chunks.

2. Fill a medium saucepan with about 1 inch of water and bring to a simmer. Place the peach in a steamer basket, set it over the simmering water, cover, and cook until tender, about 5 minutes. Allow to cool.

3. In a blender or food processor, purée the cooled peach, pumpkin purée, and chicken until the desired consistency is reached. Add water if necessary.

STORAGE: Leftover purée can be refrigerated in an airtight container for up to 3 days or frozen for up to 3 months.

NOTES

Turkey, Kale, and Papaya Purée

MAKES 6 SERVINGS, ¼ CUP EACH
PREP TIME: 5 MINUTES • COOK TIME: 15 MINUTES

Similar in flavor to chicken, but less likely to dry out when cooked in ground form, turkey is another great source of protein and iron. Unlike with beef, you may find that you need about a teaspoon of olive oil in the bottom of the pan while sautéing. The enzymes in the papaya will help your baby digest the meat and the antioxidant- and fiber-rich kale.

Variation: *Try adding brown rice or quinoa for a more complete meal, or prepare pasta stars (also known as pastina) and stir them into the turkey mixture. Babies love pastina, which cooks quickly and is extremely easy to digest.*

1 teaspoon olive oil

½ pound ground turkey

1 cup torn kale leaves

½ cup diced papaya

1. In a medium sauté pan or skillet, heat the olive oil over medium-high heat.

2. Add the ground turkey and reduce the heat to medium-low. Cook, stirring frequently and breaking up the turkey into small pieces with a spoon as it browns, for about 15 minutes, until browned evenly and cooked through.

3. While the turkey is cooking, fill a medium saucepan with about 1 inch of water and bring to a simmer. Place the kale in a steamer basket, set it over the simmering water, cover, and cook until tender, about 8 minutes. Allow to cool.

4. Drain the excess fat from the pan and allow the turkey to cool.

5. In a blender or food processor, purée the cooled turkey and kale and the papaya until the desired consistency is reached. Add water if necessary.

STORAGE: Leftover purée can be refrigerated in an airtight container for up to 3 days or frozen for up to 3 months.

NOTES

Turkey, Cauliflower, and Apricot Purée

DAIRY-FREE **NUT-FREE** GLUTEN-FREE

MAKES 4 SERVINGS, ¼ CUP EACH
PREP TIME: 5 MINUTES • COOK TIME: 15 MINUTES

Mellower than a peach or nectarine, but with a slight mouth-puckering tang, apricots make a lively accompaniment to most poultry dishes. Cauliflower, meanwhile, is as versatile a veggie as they come—and did you know that the "flowers" are actually called curds? Neither too strong nor too bland, this medley of flavors is sure to be a hit with even the pickiest of eaters.

Variation: *Since turkey and cauliflower are mild in flavor, almost any fruit can be substituted for the apricots. If apricots are out of season, try using steamed apples, steamed or very ripe pears, or ripe bananas. Around Thanksgiving, you can even try blending in a little all-natural, low-sugar cranberry sauce!*

1 teaspoon olive oil

½ pound ground turkey

1 medium apricot, pitted

½ cup cauliflower florets

1. In a medium sauté pan or skillet, heat the olive oil over medium-high heat.

2. Add the ground turkey and reduce the heat to medium-low. Cook, stirring frequently and breaking up the turkey into small pieces with a spoon as it browns, for about 15 minutes, until browned evenly and cooked through.

3. While the turkey is cooking, cut the apricot into slices.

4. Fill a medium saucepan with about 1 inch of water and bring to a simmer. Place the cauliflower in a steamer basket, set it over simmering water, cover, and cook until tender, about 12 minutes. Add the apricot during the last 5 minutes of cooking if it's not quite ripe. Allow to cool.

(Continued)

5. Drain the excess fat from the pan with the turkey and allow the turkey to cool.

6. In a blender or food processor, purée the cooled turkey, cauliflower, and apricot until the desired consistency is reached. Add water if necessary.

STORAGE: Leftover purée can be refrigerated in an airtight container for up to 3 days or frozen for up to 3 months.

NOTES

Turkey, Peas, and Apple Purée

DAIRY-FREE **NUT-FREE** GLUTEN-FREE

MAKES 4 SERVINGS, ¼ CUP EACH
PREP TIME: 5 MINUTES • COOK TIME: 15 MINUTES

Think of this as a puréed version of Thanksgiving dinner: turkey, veggies, and apple pie, minus the crust! Lighter than ground beef but just as quick cooking and easy to prepare, ground turkey is high in B vitamins and protein, and organic varieties are rich in omega-3 fatty acids. When your baby is ready for a chewier experience, this medley can be mashed with a fork instead of blended. Just be sure to steam the apple and peas until they're adequately soft.

Variation: *Try pear, mango, or papaya instead of the apple in this recipe. Pears will add a mild flavor similar to apples, while mango or papaya will give the turkey and peas a tropical twist. Steam pears as you would the apples, but there's no need to cook mango or papaya.*

1 teaspoon olive oil

½ pound ground turkey

1 large apple, cored and peeled

½ cup fresh or frozen peas

1. In a medium sauté pan or skillet, heat the olive oil over medium heat.

2. Add the ground turkey and reduce the heat to medium-low. Cook, stirring frequently and breaking up the turkey into small pieces with a spoon as it browns, for about 15 minutes, until browned evenly and cooked through.

3. While the turkey is cooking, cut the apple into 1-inch cubes.

4. Fill a medium saucepan with about 1 inch of water and bring to a simmer. Place the apple and peas in a steamer basket, set it over the simmering water, cover, and cook until tender, 5 to 8 minutes. Allow to cool.

(Continued)

5. Drain the excess fat from the pan with the turkey and allow the turkey to cool.

6. In a blender or food processor, purée the cooled turkey, apple, and peas until the desired consistency is reached. Add water if necessary.

STORAGE: Leftover purée can be refrigerated in an airtight container for up to 3 days or frozen for up to 3 months.

NOTES

Pork, Cherries, and Pears Purée

DAIRY-FREE **GLUTEN-FREE** **NUT-FREE**

MAKES 5 SERVINGS, ¼ CUP EACH
PREP TIME: 5 MINUTES • COOK TIME: 10 MINUTES

A tantalizing mix of tart and sweet, this recipe might remind you of a gourmet chutney served alongside pork chops or a roast. Your little one will love the sweet, jamlike taste, while you'll love the healthy dose of protein, antioxidants, fiber, and vitamin C this dish provides. (If you have particularly ripe, juicy cherries in the refrigerator, feel free to skip the steaming step.)

Variation: *Fruit-sweetened, premade cranberry sauce makes a tangy, super-nutritious substitute for the cherries in this recipe. Use about ¼ cup in place of the cherries. Because they can take up to 25 minutes to cook (and because they're somewhat bitter on their own) cranberries can be tricky to incorporate into baby's diet—but since they're high in antioxidants and promote urinary tract health, it's worth trying to sneak them in whenever you can.*

1 medium pear, cored and peeled

½ cup cherries, pitted and halved

½ cup diced cooked pork loin

1. Cut the pear into ½-inch cubes.

2. Fill a medium saucepan with about 1 inch of water and bring to a simmer. Place the pear and cherries in a steamer basket, set it over the simmering water, cover, and cook until tender when pierced with a fork or knife, 8 to 10 minutes. Allow to cool.

3. In a blender or food processor, purée the cooled cherries and pear and the pork until the desired consistency is reached. Add water if necessary.

STORAGE: Leftover purée can be refrigerated in an airtight container for up to 3 days or frozen for up to 3 months.

NOTES

Beef and Carrot Purée

SUPERFOOD DAIRY-FREE **NUT-FREE** GLUTEN-FREE

MAKES 4 SERVINGS, ¼ CUP EACH
PREP TIME: 5 MINUTES • COOK TIME: 15 MINUTES

Like chicken, beef is high in protein—and even higher in iron—as well as calcium, folate, and B vitamins. Stick with ground beef that's at least 80 percent lean, and look for organic or grass-fed varieties, which are higher in omega-3 fatty acids than corn-fed beef.

Variation: *If your baby has tried onions without any digestive difficulties (read: gas), try sautéing about ¼ cup diced yellow onion with the beef. A small amount of onion packs a huge helping of flavor.*

1 large carrot, peeled   ½ pound ground beef

1. Cut the carrot into ½-inch rounds.

2. Fill a medium saucepan with about 1 inch of water and bring to a simmer. Place the carrots in a steamer basket, set it over the simmering water, cover, and cook until tender, about 8 minutes. Allow to cool.

3. While the carrots are steaming, in a medium sauté pan or skillet, cook the ground beef over medium-low heat, stirring frequently and breaking the beef into small pieces with a spoon as it browns, for about 15 minutes, until browned evenly and cooked through.

4. Drain the excess fat from the pan and allow the beef to cool.

5. In a blender or food processor, purée the cooled beef and carrots until the desired consistency is reached. Add water if necessary.

STORAGE: Leftover purée can be refrigerated in an airtight container for up to 3 days or frozen for up to 3 months.

NOTES _____

_____

_____

Beef, Asparagus, and Pear Purée

DAIRY-FREE **NUT-FREE** GLUTEN-FREE

MAKES 4 SERVINGS, ¼ CUP EACH
PREP TIME: 5 MINUTES • COOK TIME: 15 MINUTES

This sweet and savory meal has all of your flavor bases covered—not to mention your baby's nutrient needs: protein, iron, fiber, folate, and vitamins A, B, and C. Asparagus also contains the "prebiotic" inulin, a type of carbohydrate that helps maintain a healthy balance of bacteria in the digestive system, particularly when paired with foods containing probiotics, such as yogurt.

1 large pear, peeled

1 cup trimmed asparagus spears

½ pound ground beef

1. Cut the pear into 1-inch chunks.

2. Fill a medium saucepan with about 1 inch of water and bring to a simmer. Place the pear and asparagus in a steamer basket, set it over the simmering water, cover, and cook until tender, about 8 minutes. Allow to cool.

3. While the asparagus and pears are steaming, in a medium sauté pan or skillet, cook the ground beef over medium-low heat, stirring frequently and breaking the beef into small pieces with a spoon as it browns, for about 15 minutes, until browned evenly and cooked through.

4. Drain the excess fat from the pan and allow the beef to cool.

5. In a blender or food processor, purée the cooled beef, pears, and asparagus until the desired consistency is reached. Add water if necessary.

STORAGE: Leftover purée can be refrigerated in an airtight container for up to 3 days or frozen for up to 3 months.

NOTES

Beef, Zucchini, and Cherries Purée

DAIRY-FREE NUT-FREE GLUTEN-FREE

MAKES 4 SERVINGS, ¼ CUP EACH
PREP TIME: 5 MINUTES • COOK TIME: 15 MINUTES

Believe it or not, cherries and beef make for a very successful pairing; you may have experienced the combination in the form of cherry-glazed brisket or burgers with black cherry compote. In this recipe, steamed zucchini adds a velvety accent to the mix.

Tip: *Use frozen cherries if you don't have time to take out the pits, or if fresh cherries aren't in season. Frozen cherries will give the purée a more watery consistency; they may need to be steamed for a minute or two longer, too.*

1 medium zucchini

½ cup cherries, pitted and halved

½ pound ground beef

1. Cut the zucchini into 1-inch chunks.

2. Fill a medium saucepan with about 1 inch of water and bring to a simmer. Place the zucchini and cherries in a steamer basket, set it over the simmering water, cover, and cook until tender, about 8 minutes. Allow to cool.

3. While the zucchini and cherries are steaming, cook the ground beef over medium-low heat in a medium sauté pan or skillet, stirring frequently and breaking the beef into small pieces with a spoon as it browns, for about 15 minutes, until browned evenly and cooked through.

4. Drain the excess fat from the pan and allow the beef to cool.

5. In a blender or food processor, purée the cooled beef, cherries, and zucchini until the desired consistency is reached. Add water if necessary.

STORAGE: Leftover purée can be refrigerated in an airtight container for up to 3 days or frozen for up to 3 months.

NOTES

Beef, Green Beans, and Prunes Purée

MAKES 4 SERVINGS, ¼ CUP EACH
PREP TIME: 5 MINUTES • COOK TIME: 15 MINUTES

While prunes are really just dried plums, they have a much richer flavor and denser texture than their fresh counterparts. They're also known for aiding babies (and adults) who are suffering from slow digestion. Save some time by looking for pitted prunes, and stick with varieties that haven't been preserved with sulfites, if possible. The sticky sweetness of this dried fruit brings out the savory quality of the browned beef in this recipe; the green beans add extra vitamins and fiber.

1 cup trimmed green beans

½ pound ground beef

¼ cup prune purée (see page 31)

1. Fill a medium saucepan with about 1 inch of water and bring to a simmer. Place the green beans in a steamer basket, set it over the simmering water, cover, and cook until tender, about 8 minutes. Allow to cool.

2. While the green beans are steaming, cook the ground beef over medium-low heat in a medium sauté pan or skillet, stirring frequently and breaking the beef into small pieces with a spoon as it browns, for about 15 minutes, until browned evenly and cooked through.

3. Drain the excess fat from the pan and allow the beef to cool.

4. In a blender or food processor, purée the cooled beef and green beans and the prune purée until the desired consistency is reached. Add water if necessary.

STORAGE: Leftover purée can be refrigerated in an airtight container for up to 3 days or frozen for up to 3 months.

NOTES

Avocado Toast

SUPERFOOD DAIRY-FREE **NUT-FREE** VEGAN

MAKES 1 SERVING

PREP TIME: 5 MINUTES • COOK TIME: 2 MINUTES

While this recipe is about as simple as they come, there's something incredibly delicious about avocado on toast—try it and you might even find yourself skipping that buttered bagel most mornings in favor of this super-healthy combo. Your avocado must be ripe enough to easily mash with a fork for this recipe to work; a purée would be much too runny.

Variation: *Try sprinkling ground flax meal, wheat germ, or a little grated cheese on top of the mashed avocado. A layer of canned refried beans also works well. You can even try adding a bit of raw tofu mashed in with the avocado for extra protein!*

1 slice whole-grain bread

½ medium avocado, halved, pitted, and peeled

1. Lightly toast the bread.

2. In a small bowl, mash the avocado with a fork.

3. Spread the avocado on the toast and cut into bite-size pieces.

STORAGE: Avocado toast should be eaten immediately.

NOTES

Applesauce Muffins

DAIRY-FREE **NUT-FREE** **VEGETARIAN**

MAKES 12 MINI MUFFINS
PREP TIME: 5 MINUTES • COOK TIME: 15 MINUTES

If you make these light and naturally sweet applesauce muffins for your child, just be prepared—she might not want to eat anything else! The key to their airy quality is the whole-wheat pastry flour, which is finer than regular whole-wheat flour, but more nutritious than white flour.

Variation: *If your child has an egg allergy or you're a vegan, substitute one large, mashed banana for the egg. It makes the muffins slightly more spongy in texture, but won't affect the cooking time.*

¼ cup plus 1 teaspoon olive oil

1 large egg

½ cup applesauce or apple purée (see page 30)

1 cup whole-wheat pastry flour

2 teaspoons baking powder

Dash ground cinnamon

1. Preheat the oven to 400°F. Grease 12 wells of a mini muffin tin with 1 teaspoon of the olive oil.

2. In a medium bowl, whisk together the remaining ¼ cup olive oil, the egg, and the applesauce. Stir in the flour, baking powder, and cinnamon.

3. Pour the mixture into the muffin cups until each is about two-thirds full Bake for 15 minutes.

4. Cut each muffin into smaller pieces before serving.

STORAGE: Leftover muffins can be stored at room temperature in an airtight container for up to 2 days, refrigerated for up to 1 week, or frozen for up to 3 months.

NOTES _____

_____

_____

Roasted Sweet Potato Nibbles

DAIRY-FREE **NUT-FREE** GLUTEN-FREE VEGAN

MAKES 5 SERVINGS, ¼ CUP EACH
PREP TIME: 5 MINUTES • COOK TIME: 25 MINUTES

As close to a dessert as any vegetable can get, this naturally sugary root vegetable is even more enticing when it's roasted, becoming caramelized and almost syrupy sweet. While most roasted veggie recipes can take close to an hour to complete, this one takes less than half the time; the sweet potatoes are cut into bite-size chunks before baking, so they cook faster and more evenly. These nibbles are equally appetizing warm, cold, or at room temperature.

Variation: *Try replacing the sweet potatoes with diced peeled butternut squash when it's in season. Squash is a wonderful substitute because it's just as tasty and nutritious as sweet potatoes and cooks in the same amount of time, so you don't need to make any recipe adjustments.*

2 medium sweet potatoes, peeled   1 tablespoon olive oil

1. Preheat the oven to 400°F.

2. Chop the sweet potatoes into ¼-inch cubes and place them in a medium bowl. Add the olive oil and stir to coat.

3. Spread the sweet potatoes in a single layer in a 9-by-13-inch baking pan, leaving about 1 inch of space between them.

4. Bake for 25 minutes, or until the sweet potatoes are tender.

STORAGE: Leftover nibbles can be refrigerated in an airtight container for up to 3 days or frozen for up to 3 months.

NOTES ————————————————————————————————

——

——

——

Tofu Bites

DAIRY-FREE **NUT-FREE** GLUTEN-FREE VEGAN

MAKES 4 SERVINGS, ¼ CUP EACH
PREP TIME: 10 MINUTES

Easy to chew and high in calcium, fiber, and fatty acids, tofu makes a fabulous first finger food. It's also considered to be a "complete protein," or a food that contains an adequate proportion of all nine of the essential amino acids necessary for a healthy diet. The ground flax meal offers its own heart-healthy, antioxidizing nutrients—plus, the texture of the meal makes the slippery tofu easier for little fingers to pick up.

Variation: *The texture of raw tofu might be off-putting to some babies—or even to you! For a sweet treat that's likely to be gobbled up, replace the tofu in this recipe with slices of banana; just make sure they're not too mushy.*

1 (14-ounce) package firm tofu, drained   2 tablespoons ground flax meal

1. Cut the tofu into 1-inch cubes.

2. In a small bowl or a large zip-top bag, combine the tofu with the flax meal. Mix or shake until the cubes are evenly coated.

   STORAGE: Leftover bites can be refrigerated in an airtight container for up to 2 days.

   NOTES

Fun-Size Asparagus Frittatas

NUT-FREE **GLUTEN-FREE** **VEGETARIAN**

MAKES 12 MINI MUFFIN FRITTATAS

PREP TIME: 5 MINUTES • COOK TIME: 12 TO 14 MINUTES

While pediatricians once advised holding off on introducing eggs to your child until up to two years of age, according to the most recent recommendations from the American Academy of Pediatrics, offering eggs as early as six months is not only acceptable, but might even help prevent food allergies from developing. Eggs are a good source of easily digestible protein and contain many other essential nutrients such as choline, vitamin D, and folate. Look for cage-free or organic varieties.

Cooking Tip: *The best muffin liners around are made of parchment paper not only because they pop easily out of muffin tins, but also food pops easily out of the liners.*

1 teaspoon olive oil

3 large eggs

2 tablespoons grated cheddar cheese

¼ cup diced asparagus

1. Preheat the oven to 375°F. Grease 12 wells of a mini muffin tin with the olive oil.

2. Crack the eggs into a medium bowl and whisk. Whisk in the cheese. Add the asparagus and stir.

3. Pour the mixture into the muffin cups until each is about two-thirds full.

4. Bake for 12 to 14 minutes.

5. Cut each frittata into smaller pieces before serving.

STORAGE: Leftover frittatas can be refrigerated in an airtight container for up to 2 days.

NOTES _____

_____

_____

_____

Turkey and Cheese Quesadillas

NUT-FREE GLUTEN-FREE

MAKES 2 SERVINGS

PREP TIME: 5 MINUTES • COOK TIME: 5 MINUTES

While traditional cold cuts are loaded with nitrates and other unhealthy fillers, organic deli meats are a useful shortcut for busy parents in search of a quick, kid-friendly protein fix. They're also easy for little toothless ones to chew, particularly when cut into small bites as instructed in this recipe. Look for organic turkey breast, as well as organic corn tortillas, to make sure there are no GMOs in your food.

Variation: *This is a versatile, if simple, recipe that works well with various meats. In place of the turkey, try organic sliced ham for a sweeter flavor or roast beef for a richer taste.*

2 slices turkey breast meat

¼ cup shredded cheddar cheese

2 small corn tortillas

1. Layer the turkey on one of the tortillas and sprinkle with the cheese. Place the other tortilla over it to cover.

2. In a medium sauté pan or skillet, cook the quesadilla over medium heat until the cheese has melted, about 2 minutes on each side.

3. Allow the quesadilla to cool a little, then cut into bite-size pieces.

STORAGE: Leftover quesadilla can be wrapped in plastic wrap and refrigerated for up to 1 day.

NOTES

Broccoli and Carrot Pancakes

SUPERFOOD DAIRY-FREE NUT-FREE VEGAN

MAKES 8 TO 10 SILVER DOLLAR–SIZE PANCAKES
PREP TIME: 5 MINUTES • COOK TIME: 20 MINUTES

Kids love pancakes, and these veggie-filled flapjacks are no exception. Hold the butter and maple syrup—thanks to the carrots and applesauce, these pancakes are sweet enough without any added sugar.

Variation: *Nearly any veggies can be used in place of the broccoli and carrots; just be sure to steam them to the point where they're soft enough to mash easily with a fork.*

¼ cup broccoli florets

¼ cup diced peeled carrot

1 cup whole-wheat pastry flour

1 cup water

1 tablespoon applesauce

1 teaspoon olive oil

1. Fill a medium saucepan with about 1 inch of water, and bring to a simmer. Place the broccoli and carrot in a steamer basket, set it over the simmering water, cover, and cook until very tender, about 15 minutes. Allow to cool.

2. Transfer the broccoli and carrot to a medium bowl, and mash with a fork.

3. Add the flour, water, and applesauce, and stir to combine.

4. In a large sauté pan or skillet, heat the olive oil over medium heat.

5. Pour small circles of the batter (about 3 inches in diameter) into the pan. When bubbles appear on one side, flip the pancakes with a spatula and cook until golden brown on both sides.

6. Cut the pancakes into small pieces to serve.

STORAGE: Leftover pancakes can be refrigerated in an airtight container for up to 1 day.

NOTES

Sweet Potato and Bean Balls

SUPERFOOD   DAIRY-FREE   **NUT-FREE**   GLUTEN-FREE   VEGAN

MAKES ABOUT 10 BALLS
PREP TIME: 5 MINUTES

Kids love putting small, fun-shaped items in their mouths. Luckily, these little treats are much tastier and more nutritious than most things your baby will try to eat! They're also soft and easy to chew, with a texture that's not too mushy and not too chunky. Savory and sweet, these bean balls are great on their own or served with applesauce or another fruit purée for dipping.

Tip: *High in fiber, protein, and antioxidants, cannellini beans have a buttery, mellow flavor and skins that aren't quite as tough as other varieties of beans, such as red kidney beans. Rinsing canned beans after draining them can help prevent the gassy side effects associated with legumes.*

1 cup canned cannellini beans, drained and rinsed

½ cup sweet potato purée (see page 33)

¼ cup ground flax meal

1. Place the beans in a medium bowl and mash well with a fork.

2. Add the sweet potato purée and flax meal to the bowl and mix well to combine.

3. Using a spoon, scoop about 1 tablespoon of the mixture and form it into a ball with your hands. Repeat until you have used all of the mixture.

STORAGE: Leftover bean balls can be refrigerated in an airtight container for up to 2 days or frozen for up to 3 months.

NOTES

Baked Pear Slices

GLUTEN-FREE　DAIRY-FREE　**NUT-FREE**　VEGAN

MAKES 6 TO 8 SLICES

PREP TIME: 5 MINUTES • COOK TIME: 15 MINUTES

Baking pear slices not only brings out the natural sweetness of the fruit, but also makes the slices easier to chew. This method works well for turning other hard fruits into finger foods, too, such as apples or stone fruits (peaches, nectarines, and plums) that aren't soft enough. If baking stone fruits, however, leave the skins on and remove them after they're cooked.

Variation: *Try adding a sprinkle of cinnamon or nutmeg before baking. This is also great on apples, peaches, nectarines, and plums.*

1 large pear, cored and peeled   2 ½ tablespoons water

1. Preheat the oven to 350°F.

2. Cut the pear into slices and spread them in a single layer in a 9-by-11-inch glass baking dish, leaving about 1 inch between the slices.

3. Pour the water over the pears.

4. Bake until the pears are tender, about 15 minutes.

5. Cut each slice into smaller pieces before serving.

   STORAGE: Leftover slices can be refrigerated in an airtight container for up to 2 days.

   NOTES ————————————————————————————————

   ——

   ——

   ——

Apple Date Bars

DAIRY-FREE **NUT-FREE** **VEGAN**

MAKES 6 TO 8 SLICES

PREP TIME: 5 MINUTES • COOK TIME: 20 MINUTES

Just as decadent and rich as oatmeal cookies but without the added sugar or refined flour, these yummy bars are packed with fiber and protein. They make an excellent breakfast or snack and are particularly portable; toss a few in an insulated bag and bring them to the playground for when your little one needs a quick energy fix—and bring a few extra for yourself!

Tip: *High in fiber, iron, and potassium, dates are as sweet as candy—and just as sticky, too! To keep this gooey quality from making them too difficult to chop, try coating a pair of kitchen shears or a sharp knife with cooking spray or olive oil.*

Cooking spray

1½ cups quick-cooking rolled oats

¼ cup whole-wheat pastry flour

⅔ cup chopped pitted dates

1½ cups grated apple

¼ cup apple juice

1. Preheat the oven to 400°F. Coat an 8-by-8-inch glass baking dish with cooking spray.

2. In a large bowl, combine the oats, flour, dates, apple, and apple juice, and stir well to combine.

3. Press the mixture into the baking dish in an even layer. Bake until lightly browned, about 20 minutes.

4. Allow the bars to cool slightly before cutting into bite-size pieces.

STORAGE: Leftover bars can be refrigerated in an airtight container for up to 1 week or frozen for up to 3 months.

NOTES

Cottage Cheese and Kiwi

SUPERFOOD NUT-FREE GLUTEN-FREE VEGETARIAN

MAKES 1 SERVING, ½ CUP
PREP TIME: 5 MINUTES

Once popular as a diet food, cottage cheese—the full-fat variety—is actually a convenient and delicious way to sneak extra calcium and protein into your baby's diet. Most little ones like the taste and texture all by itself, but combining cottage cheese with a juicy, colorful fruit like kiwi adds to its appeal and nutritional content.

Variation: *You can try as many different spins on this variation as there are fruits in the supermarket; they all make for quick and tasty snacks or even breakfasts. Soft, tropical fruits like papaya, honeydew, cantaloupe, and watermelon mix especially well with cottage cheese.*

1 medium kiwi, peeled   ¼ cup full-fat cottage cheese

1. Chop the kiwi into ½-inch cubes.

2. In a small bowl, combine the cottage cheese and kiwi.

   STORAGE: Cottage cheese and kiwi should be eaten right away.

   NOTES ———————————————————————————

Strawberry-Papaya Yogurt Mix-Ins

SUPERFOOD   NUT-FREE   GLUTEN-FREE   VEGETARIAN

MAKES 5 SERVINGS, ¼ CUP EACH
PREP TIME: 5 MINUTES

High in calcium and protein, yogurt contains live, active cultures that can help maintain healthy bacteria in baby's digestive tract. Be sure to avoid yogurts that say "heat treated" on the label, as is the case with many commercially prepared yogurts; this process destroys the beneficial cultures. Rather than buying fruit-flavored yogurts, which often contain added sugars, make your own by adding fresh, diced fruit or fruit purées to full-fat plain yogurt.

Variation: *Add any diced soft fruit to your baby's yogurt. Bananas, peaches, mangos, and kiwi work especially well.*

¼ cup diced strawberries

¼ cup diced papaya

1 (6-ounce) container full-fat plain yogurt

In a medium bowl, mix the strawberries, papaya, and yogurt together.

STORAGE: Leftover yogurt can be stored in the refrigerator in an airtight container for up to 2 days.

NOTES

Confetti Couscous

SUPERFOOD **NUT-FREE** **VEGETARIAN**

MAKES 4 SERVINGS, ¼ CUP EACH
PREP TIME: 5 MINUTES • COOK TIME: 10 MINUTES

Often mistaken for a grain, couscous is actually a type of pasta. Still, the small, grain-like texture makes it easier for babies to chew than even the tiniest pasta shape. Choose whole-wheat couscous when you can; it's higher in fiber and protein than the regular variety, and baby will love the nutty (but nut-free!) flavor. Both types of couscous cook quickly. Either fresh or frozen veggies can be used in this recipe, but using frozen saves peeling and chopping time and guarantees that the carrots will all be the same size.

1 cup water

1 cup whole-wheat couscous

½ cup frozen mixed peas and carrots

2 tablespoons grated Parmesan cheese (optional)

1. In a small pot with a lid, bring the water to a boil over high heat.

2. Remove the pot from the heat, pour in the couscous, and stir.

3. Cover the pot and let it sit for 10 minutes or until all the water has been absorbed.

4. While the couscous is cooking, fill a medium saucepan with about 1 inch of water and bring to a simmer. Place the peas and carrots in a steamer basket, set it over the simmering water, cover, and cook until tender, about 5 minutes.

5. In a medium bowl, combine the couscous, peas and carrots, and Parmesan cheese, if desired.

STORAGE: Leftover couscous can be refrigerated in an airtight container for up to 2 days.

NOTES

Tasty Turkey, Sweet Potato, and Bean Stew

SUPERFOOD DAIRY-FREE NUT-FREE GLUTEN-FREE

MAKES 12 SERVINGS, ¼ CUP EACH
PREP TIME: 5 MINUTES • COOKING TIME: 25 MINUTES

Super high in both protein and fiber, this hearty stew is perfect on chilly fall and winter evenings—though it's just as yummy in the middle of spring or summer. If you have some fresh tarragon on hand, sprinkle in about a tablespoon while the stew is simmering. Delicate and fragrant, tarragon tastes a bit like fennel and goes well with white meats and all kinds of vegetables. For "dessert," try a little pure pumpkin purée spiked with cinnamon and nutmeg.

Tip: *Depending on how much texture your baby can handle, this stew can be puréed for a smoother consistency. While cannellini beans are soft, they do have skins that can be tricky for babies with no teeth to chew. Just a quick pulse in the blender or food processor will make this meal easier to manage while still retaining a nice chunky feel.*

1 tablespoon olive oil

1 pound ground turkey

1 medium sweet potato, peeled

1 can cannellini beans, drained and rinsed

2 cups low-sodium chicken or vegetable broth, or water

1. In a large stockpot, heat the olive oil over medium-high heat. Line a plate with a paper towel.

2. Add the ground turkey and sauté until browned, about 5 minutes.

3. Transfer the turkey to the paper towel–lined plate to drain.

4. Cut the sweet potato into ½-inch cubes and add them to the pot in which you browned the turkey. Cook over medium heat for about 5 minutes.

(Continued)

5. Return the turkey to the pot and add the beans and broth. Bring to a boil over high heat.

6. Reduce the heat to medium-low and simmer for about 10 minutes. Allow to cool slightly before serving.

STORAGE: Leftover stew can be refrigerated in an airtight container for up to 3 days or frozen for up to 3 months.

NOTES

Butternut Squash "Mac and Cheese"

SUPERFOOD | DAIRY-FREE | NUT-FREE | VEGETARIAN

MAKES 4 SERVINGS, ¼ CUP EACH
PREP TIME: 5 MINUTES • COOK TIME: 10 MINUTES

If your baby is allergic to cow's-milk products or your family is vegan, this dairy-free version of the classic comfort food provides more vitamin A, fiber, and folate than the original. Thanks to the mellow appeal of the butternut squash and full flavor of the whole-wheat pasta, your baby won't even know what he's missing. Of course, cheese can easily be added to this recipe if you'd prefer; simply stir in about a tablespoon of grated Parmesan cheese after the recipe's final step.

Variation: *Make this pasta a more complete meal by adding steamed peas or diced cooked chicken breast. The peas will bring texture, color, and nutrition to the dish; the chicken's savory quality will cut the sweetness of the butternut squash nicely while adding protein.*

3 cups water

1 cup whole-wheat elbow macaroni

½ cup frozen cooked butternut squash purée, thawed

1. In a large pot, bring the water to a boil over high heat.

2. Add the pasta, reduce the heat to medium, and cook for 8 to 10 minutes, or until tender. Drain the pasta in a colander.

3. In a medium bowl, combine the warm pasta with the thawed squash purée.

STORAGE: Leftover "Mac and Cheese" can be refrigerated in an airtight container for up to 2 days.

NOTES

Tofu, Quinoa, and Avocado Bowl

SUPERFOOD   DAIRY-FREE   NUT-FREE   GLUTEN-FREE   VEGAN

MAKES 6 SERVINGS, ¼ CUP EACH
PREP TIME: 5 MINUTES • COOK TIME: 15 MINUTES

This total nutrition trifecta combines three of the healthiest foods for your baby, all of which happen to be especially easy to chew. Make an extra portion for yourself and add a touch of low-sodium soy sauce or tamari. Sea kelp flakes also make a delicious addition and provide iron, calcium, and magnesium; you can shake a few of these onto your baby's bowl, too.

Variation: *Cooked brown rice can be substituted for the quinoa in this dish if you have extra time on your hands or leftover rice in the refrigerator. Rice will give this dish a creamier consistency and pairs well with both tofu and avocado. Think of it as vegetarian sushi in a bowl!*

1 cup water

½ cup quinoa

½ cup diced avocado

½ cup diced firm tofu

1. In a pot with a lid, bring the water to boil over high heat.

2. Add the quinoa and cover the pot. Reduce the heat to low and simmer for about 15 minutes, or until the water has been absorbed. Remove from the heat and allow the quinoa to cool.

3. In a medium bowl, combine the cooled quinoa, avocado, and tofu, and stir gently.

STORAGE: Leftovers can be refrigerated in an airtight container for up to 2 days or frozen for up to 3 months.

NOTES

Mini Apple-Turkey Meatballs

DAIRY-FREE   **NUT-FREE**

MAKES ABOUT 20 MINI MEATBALLS
PREP TIME: 10 MINUTES • COOK TIME: 15 MINUTES

These wonderfully simple meatballs hide a nutritious surprise—apples! Delicious on their own or served over pasta (try them with Butternut Squash "Mac and Cheese," page 121), these versatile treats are also yummy dipped into full-fat plain yogurt blended with a touch of cinnamon. Or for a more savory experience, add a teaspoon of dried oregano to the meat-and-apple mixture.

Tip: *Try grating the apple it for babies who prefer their food to have a smoother texture. Other grated fruits and veggies can easily be hidden in meatballs, too; try pears for a mellow flavor similar to apples, or zucchini for a meal that's not so sweet.*

Olive oil or cooking spray (optional)

1 small apple, cored and peeled

1 cup whole-wheat bread crumbs

1½ pounds ground turkey

2 large eggs

1. Preheat the oven to 425°F. Line a 9-by-13-inch baking sheet with parchment paper, or grease it with olive oil or cooking spray.

2. Dice the apple and place it in a large bowl. Add the bread crumbs, turkey, and eggs, and stir to combine—do not overmix.

3. Using your hands, roll the mixture into tablespoon balls and place them 1 inch apart from each other on the prepared baking sheet. Bake for 15 minutes, or until cooked through.

4. Allow to cool. Cut into smaller pieces before serving.

STORAGE: Leftover meatballs can be refrigerated in an airtight container for up to 2 days or frozen for up to 3 months.

NOTES

Leftover Chicken and Brown Rice with Sautéed Kale

DAIRY-FREE   **NUT-FREE**   **GLUTEN-FREE**

MAKES 3 SERVINGS, ⅓ CUP EACH
PREP TIME: 5 MINUTES • COOK TIME: 7 MINUTES

Having leftovers in the refrigerator (or freezer) pays off when it comes to this recipe, which uses several separately cooked ingredients to make one full meal. While some babies between nine and eleven months might be ready to tackle these textures before this dish is blended, others might need a smoother consistency. Use your judgment and start with small spoonfuls.

Variation: *Experiment with other combinations of cooked meats, grains, and greens. Beef, barley, and collard greens make a hearty, iron-rich meal, while turkey, Swiss chard, and quinoa combine for a lighter but still nutrient-dense dinner.*

½ cup cooked brown rice

½ cup diced cooked chicken breast

¼ cup sautéed kale purée (see page 53)

1. In a small saucepan, combine the cooked brown rice and kale purée.

2. Cook over medium heat until both ingredients are warmed through and mixed well, 4 to 5 minutes.

3. Add the diced chicken and cook for about 2 minutes more.

4. Transfer the mixture to a blender or food processor, and blend until the desired consistency is reached.

STORAGE: Leftovers can be refrigerated in an airtight container for up to 2 days or frozen for up to 3 months.

NOTES

Easy Black Bean and Zucchini Soup

DAIRY-FREE **NUT-FREE** GLUTEN-FREE VEGAN

MAKES 3 SERVINGS, ⅓ CUP EACH
PREP TIME: 5 MINUTES • COOK TIME: 20 MINUTES

A Mexican restaurant menu favorite, black bean soup is high in protein, folate, fiber, and antioxidants—not to mention flavor! The buttery zucchini in this recipe is a perfect complement to the smoky quality of the beans.

Variation: *For a sweeter soup, the zucchini can be replaced with diced carrots. In this case, however, you'll need to sauté the carrots a little longer, 8 to 10 minutes. If your baby tolerates dairy, just add a bit of sour cream, yogurt, or grated cheese at the end for a richer flavor.*

1 medium zucchini

1 teaspoon olive oil

1 (15-ounce) can black beans, drained and rinsed

1½ cups low-sodium vegetable broth

1. Chop the zucchini into ¼-inch chunks.

2. In a large saucepan, heat the olive oil over medium heat.

3. Sauté the zucchini until tender, about 5 minutes.

4. Add the beans and broth to the pan and bring to a boil. Reduce the heat to low and simmer for about 15 minutes.

5. Using an immersion blender, purée the soup directly in the pot, or working in batches, transfer the soup to a standing blender and purée.

STORAGE: Leftover black bean soup can be stored in the refrigerator in an airtight container for up to 3 days or for up to 3 months in the freezer.

NOTES ————————————————————————————

——

——

——

Mini Meat Loaf Muffins

SUPERFOOD DAIRY-FREE NUT-FREE

MAKES ABOUT 24 MINI MEAT LOAF MUFFINS
PREP TIME: 10 MINUTES • COOK TIME: 15 MINUTES

Making this meat loaf in a mini muffin version means it cooks in less than half the time of your grandma's famous loaf. If your baby has a tendency to shove huge bites of food into his mouth, quarter these muffins before serving. Boost the nutritional value of this diner staple by adding beta-carotene-packed grated carrots to grass-fed organic beef.

Variation: *Because of the tomato's acidic and allergenic properties, some parents prefer to wait until the age of one year to introduce it to their baby. When your little one is ready, however, a tablespoon of tomato sauce mixed into the meat gives this recipe a more classic meat loaf flavor, plus extra lycopene and vitamin C.*

2 teaspoons olive oil

1 medium carrot, peeled

1 pound ground beef

½ cup whole-wheat bread crumbs

1 large egg

1. Preheat the oven to 425°F. Grease a standard mini muffin tin with the olive oil.

2. On the large holes of a box grater, shred the carrot.

3. In a large bowl, combine the carrot, beef, bread crumbs, and egg, and stir well to combine—do not overmix.

4. Drop tablespoons of the meat mixture into the wells of the muffin tin.

5. Bake until the meat loaf muffins are browned and cooked through, about 15 minutes.

STORAGE: Leftover meat loaf muffins can be refrigerated in an airtight container for up to 2 days or frozen for up to 3 months.

NOTES

Alphabet and Veggie Pasta

SUPERFOOD DAIRY-FREE **NUT-FREE** VEGAN

MAKES 8 SERVINGS, ¼ CUP EACH
PREP TIME: 5 MINUTES • COOK TIME: 10 MINUTES

Your baby might be too young to read, but she's not too young to appreciate colorful, tiny letters and numbers! Alphabet pasta is also easy to chew; mixed with the array of veggies in this recipe, it makes for a healthy, well-rounded meal that can be on the table in minutes.

Variation: *Once your baby has been introduced to tomatoes—usually around her first birthday—you may want to try tossing the cooked pasta and veggies in ¼ cup warm marinara sauce. Sprinkle a couple of teaspoons of grated Parmesan cheese on top, and you'll have an Italian-style dinner for the whole family!*

3 cups water

1 cup alphabet shapes pasta

½ cup diced zucchini

½ cup diced carrot

½ cup fresh or frozen peas

1. In a large pot, bring the water to a boil over high heat.

2. Add the pasta and reduce the heat to medium. Cook until the pasta is tender, about 8 minutes. Drain the pasta in a colander.

3. While the pasta is cooking, fill a medium saucepan with about 1 inch of water and bring to a simmer. Place the zucchini, carrot, and peas in a steamer basket, set it over the simmering water, cover, and cook until tender, 8 to 10 minutes. Allow to cool.

4. Place the pasta and veggies in a large bowl and toss to combine.

STORAGE: Leftover pasta can be refrigerated in an airtight container for up to 2 days.

NOTES

Real Meals and Snacks

· ·

Your baby is officially a toddler now—and they don't call them "toddlers" for nothing. Whether she's walking, cruising, crawling, or some combination of all three, your little one probably spends most of her time toddling these days, which means it might be tough to get her to settle down for meals. And thanks to her developing language skills, don't be surprised if she turns down your offers of breakfast or lunch with a firm "No!" Of course, she's just as likely to ask for her favorite foods, too. Luckily, she's getting much better at chewing and transferring food from her high chair tray to her mouth.

IS BABY READY?

She's already been grabbing for the spoon while you try to feed her; now she's probably ready for a spoon of her very own. True, she'll get more food on her face and in her hair than in her mouth at first, but it's important to let her practice her self-feeding skills. Work around her initial clumsiness by starting out with two spoons: one for her and one for you. Also consider investing in a suction-bottomed bowl, which is less likely to end up toppling off the high chair tray.

The "real meals" and snack recipes in this chapter will sound very much like the types of foods you'd find yourself eating throughout the day, from pancakes to soups to pizzas. The only real difference is in how small an amount goes into your baby's mouth. Your baby also might be ready for some very grown-up tastes. As long as she's tolerated the foods you've introduced so far and hasn't shown any signs of allergy, proceed, with your pediatrician's blessing.

RECOMMENDED SERVING SIZES

Between 12 and 18 months of age, your baby will probably be eating three solid meals a day plus a couple of snacks. Servings should still be about the size of your baby's fist, including:

- 1 cup fruit

- 1 cup vegetables

- 2 cups dairy (1 cup whole milk or full-fat plain yogurt plus 1½ ounces hard cheese or ⅓ cup shredded cheese)

- 2 ounces protein-rich foods (2 slices deli meat; ¼ cup cooked meat such as diced chicken breast; 1 egg; ¼ cup beans)

- 3 ounces grains (1 cup cereal; ¼ cup pasta, rice, quinoa, or couscous; 1 slice bread)

BREAST MILK OR FORMULA

Every toddler is different, but you'll probably notice a decrease in your little one's breast milk or formula consumption after his first birthday (if you haven't already). That's not to say he won't still benefit from the nutrients in your breast milk, if you choose to continue nursing; the American Academy of Pediatrics recommends breastfeeding for at least one year ("AAP Reaffirms Breastfeeding Guidelines"), while the World Health Organization advises nursing for two years or even more. Whether your baby is drinking breast milk, formula, or cow's milk, he should be getting 16 to 24 ounces a day.

INCREASING INDEPENDENCE

Don't be alarmed if your toddler eats a huge plate of food one day and barely anything the next, or if he adores peas for a week straight, then suddenly wants nothing to do with them. These inconsistencies are perfectly normal and are part of your little one's ambivalence over his increasing independence. On one hand, he wants to do things all by himself; on the other, he still wants his parents to do everything for him. There are other developmental reasons for your baby's eating habits. After a year of incredibly rapid growth and weight gain, toddlers begin to gain weight more slowly; consequently, they go through periods where they're not all that hungry. Here are some tips to help you navigate mealtimes during this phase:

- Allow your toddler to "graze" on a variety of foods by offering bite-size portions of various colorful items in an ice cube tray or a muffin tin.

- Most toddlers love dipping their food. Offer healthy dips such as yogurt, cottage cheese, or mashed avocado (or use one of the recipes on pages 198–200) with soft fruits or vegetables or pieces of whole-grain bread, pita, or rice cakes.

- Play with presentation by offering foods in fun and unexpected ways, like using colorful plates or measuring cups.

- Experiment with smoothies. For truly on-the-go toddlers, occasionally a meal in a sippy cup is the only way to sneak a little nutrition into his day. Nearly any fruit or veggie can be blended into an appetizing shake (see recipes on pages 154–155).

NEW FOODS TO INTRODUCE

At 12 months:

Citrus fruits	Honey	Spinach
Cow's milk	Nuts/nut butters (if no family history of allergy)	Tomatoes

Whole-Wheat Banana Pancakes

SUPERFOOD NUT-FREE VEGETARIAN

MAKES 8 TO 10 PANCAKES
PREP TIME: 5 MINUTES • COOK TIME: 10 MINUTES

Perfect for a weekend breakfast, these pancakes can be served to the entire family. High in fiber, protein, and potassium, this dish goes well with scrambled eggs and bacon, but it's also a complete meal all by itself.

Tip: *If your skillet or pan isn't nonstick, add a little oil or butter to the pan before making the pancakes.*

½ cup whole-wheat pastry flour

2 teaspoons baking soda

½ teaspoon salt

2 large ripe bananas, peeled

1 cup whole milk or water

1 tablespoon olive oil

1 large egg

1. In a large bowl, combine the flour, baking soda, and salt.

2. In a small bowl, mash the bananas; then stir in the milk, oil, and egg.

3. Add the banana mixture to the bowl with the flour mixture and stir until just blended.

4. Heat a large nonstick sauté pan or skillet over medium heat.

5. Pour ¼-cup portions of the pancake mixture into the pan, making a few pancakes at a time. When bubbles appear on one side, flip the pancakes over with a spatula. Cook until golden brown on both sides.

6. Cut the pancakes into smaller pieces and serve.

STORAGE: Leftover pancakes can be refrigerated in an airtight container for up to 1 day or placed between sheets of parchment paper and frozen in a freezer bag for up to 3 months.

NOTES

Breakfast Couscous

NUT-FREE **VEGETARIAN**

MAKES 4 SERVINGS, ½ CUP EACH
PREP TIME: 5 MINUTES • COOK TIME: 5 MINUTES

Oatmeal and grits aren't the only warm cereals to eat right after waking up. Rise and shine with this soothing couscous breakfast, which takes just a few minutes longer to make than instant oatmeal and provides fiber and iron, courtesy of the dried apricots. Chopped dried apricots are also a favorite tasty finger food served on their own.

Variation: *To make this naturally sweet breakfast treat gluten free, protein-packed quinoa can easily stand in for the couscous.*

2 cups water

1 cup whole milk, or soy or almond milk

1 cup whole-wheat couscous

½ cup chopped dried apricots

½ teaspoon ground cinnamon

1. In a medium saucepan, combine the water and milk and bring to a boil over medium heat.

2. Stir in the couscous, apricots, and cinnamon. Cover, remove from the heat, and let stand for 5 minutes.

STORAGE: Leftover couscous can be refrigerated in an airtight container for up to 1 day.

NOTES ———————————————————————————————

———————————————————————————————————————

———————————————————————————————————————

———————————————————————————————————————

Tofu Scramble

SUPERFOOD NUT-FREE GLUTEN-FREE VEGAN

MAKES 8 SERVINGS, ¼ CUP EACH
PREP TIME: 5 MINUTES • COOK TIME: 10 MINUTES

This vegan version of scrambled eggs is higher in calcium and fiber than the original, thanks to the main ingredient, tofu. Meanwhile, the spinach and tomatoes add lycopene, vitamin C, and some much-needed color. You can toss nearly any steamed veggies you happen to have on hand into this mix; vegetable purées can also be stirred in when the tofu is added.

Tip: *Make sure that your tofu is well drained before cooking to prevent the scramble from getting too watery. One way to do this is by pressing the tofu: Place the block of tofu in a small bowl. Layer two paper towels on top of the tofu, then put a heavy plate or bowl over the paper towels. Let the tofu sit for about 15 minutes, then drain any liquid from the bowl, crumble the tofu, and proceed with the recipe.*

1 tablespoon olive oil

½ cup diced tomato

1 cup chopped spinach

1 package firm or extra-firm tofu, drained and crumbled

1. In a large skillet, heat the olive oil over medium-high heat. Add the tomatoes and cook for 2 to 3 minutes.

2. Reduce the heat to medium-low and add the spinach and crumbled tofu.

3. Cover and cook for 5 to 7 minutes, or until the liquid has mostly evaporated.

STORAGE: Leftover tofu scramble can be refrigerated in an airtight container for up to 1 day.

NOTES

Quick Red Lentil Soup

SUPERFOOD · DAIRY-FREE · **NUT-FREE** · GLUTEN-FREE · VEGAN

MAKES 9 SERVINGS, ½ CUP EACH
PREP TIME: 5 MINUTES • COOK TIME: 18 MINUTES

High in fiber, protein, and B vitamins, red lentils cook more quickly than most varieties and are thought to be more easily digested, too. This recipe is as adult-friendly as it is pleasing to toddler palates, and makes a large batch so the entire family can dig in at dinnertime. It also freezes well, so leftovers won't go to waste.

Variation: *For added vitamins and minerals, try adding a few cups of washed baby spinach leaves to the soup as a final step; just stir them in during the final 2 minutes of cooking. If you do add the spinach, you may need to lightly purée the soup with an immersion blender so your little one doesn't choke on the stems. Even if you don't use spinach, blending the soup will give it a creamier consistency—but it's not necessary.*

1 tablespoon olive oil

4 medium carrots, peeled and diced

1 small onion, diced

1 (14½-ounce) can diced tomatoes

1½ cups low-sodium vegetable broth

1 cup dried red lentils

2 cups water

1. In a medium saucepan, heat the olive oil over medium heat. Add the carrots and onion, and cook until lightly browned and soft, about 8 minutes.

2. Add the tomatoes, broth, lentils, and water. Cover and raise the heat to high. Bring to a boil.

3. Reduce the heat to low and simmer, covered, for 8 to 10 minutes, until the lentils are tender.

STORAGE: Leftover soup can be refrigerated in an airtight container for up to 3 days or frozen for up to 3 months.

NOTES

Simple Butternut Squash Soup

SUPERFOOD **NUT-FREE** **VEGETARIAN**

MAKES 6 SERVINGS, ½ CUP EACH
PREP TIME: 5 MINUTES • COOK TIME: 7 MINUTES

Most butternut squash soups take at least an hour to prepare, but this bright orange meal in a bowl takes mere minutes to get on the table, thanks to the use of frozen purée. While the recipe calls for the use of half-and-half, you can easily make it dairy-free by substituting unsweetened soy, rice, or almond milk.

Tip: *An immersion blender is a great tool for puréeing soup because you can place it directly in the cooking pot, which means no tricky transfer of hot liquids from stove to blender or food processor. If you don't have an immersion blender, be sure to let the soup cool slightly before pouring it into your blender, and try blending in small batches so you don't end up splashing yourself with scalding soup!*

1 tablespoon olive oil
1 small onion, diced
1 tablespoon all-purpose flour
½ cup half-and-half

1½ cups low-sodium vegetable broth
1 (12-ounce) package frozen cooked
    butternut squash purée, thawed

1. In a large saucepan, heat the olive oil over medium heat. Add the onion and flour, and cook, stirring occasionally, for 3 minutes.

2. Stir in the half-and-half and broth, and cook for 2 minutes more.

3. Add the thawed squash and cook for about 2 minutes.

4. Purée the soup directly in the pot using an immersion blender, or working in batches, transfer the soup to a blender or food processor and purée.

STORAGE: Leftover soup can be refrigerated in an airtight container for up to 3 days.

NOTES

Mac and Cheese Soup

SUPERFOOD **NUT-FREE**

MAKES 6 SERVINGS, ½ CUP EACH
PREP TIME: 5 MINUTES • COOK TIME: 15 MINUTES

You can't beat macaroni and cheese for sheer kid-friendliness, but you can try to make this favorite dish a bit more nutritious—by turning it into soup, for example! This meal-in-a-bowl features fiber, vitamins, and minerals in the form of a colorful array of veggies, and the small pasta shells are perfectly bite-size. If your little one likes to dip, try serving this with a side of whole-grain bread.

Variation: *Try the same amount of frozen peas, green beans, carrots, and corn (usually sold as a mixture) in place of the broccoli, cauliflower, and carrots, or add ½ cup diced cooked chicken breast at the end for extra protein.*

1 (32-ounce) container low-sodium chicken
  broth

6 ounces small pasta shells

1 (16-ounce) bag frozen mixed broccoli,
  cauliflower, and carrots

1½ cups whole milk

1 tablespoon all-purpose flour

1½ cups shredded cheddar cheese

1. In a large saucepan, bring the broth to a boil over high heat. Add the pasta and return to a boil. Reduce the heat and simmer, uncovered, for 5 minutes.

2. Add the broccoli, cauliflower, and carrots. Cook until the pasta and vegetables are tender, about 5 minutes more.

3. Stir in the milk and flour. Cook, stirring, until thickened and bubbly, about 2 minutes.

4. Gradually add the cheese, stirring until the cheese melts.

STORAGE: Leftover soup can be refrigerated in an airtight container for up to 2 days or frozen for up to 3 months.

NOTES _____

Mozzarella Poppers

NUT-FREE **VEGETARIAN**

MAKES 12 POPPERS

PREP TIME: 10 MINUTES • COOK TIME: 5 MINUTES

A much healthier version of fast-food mozzarella sticks, these poppers are baked, not fried. Panko bread crumbs, which are made from crustless bread, are also lighter and crispier than the traditional kind and tend to absorb less grease (try them as a coating for chicken nuggets). Serve these poppers with a side of marinara sauce for dipping, if desired.

Variation: *If you're aiming for a more traditional "mozzarella stick" taste, look for Italian-seasoned panko bread crumbs. Or make your own by adding ¼ teaspoon each of dried oregano, dried thyme, and dried parsley to your bread crumbs.*

Cooking spray

1 large egg

⅓ cup panko bread crumbs

3 (1-ounce) mozzarella cheese sticks (string cheese)

1. Preheat the oven to 425°F. Line a 9-by-13-inch baking sheet with aluminum foil. Coat the foil with cooking spray.

2. Break the egg into a small bowl and beat well. Place the panko in a separate shallow bowl.

3. Cut the mozzarella sticks into 1-inch pieces. Dip one piece at a time into the beaten egg, then dredge in the panko. Place the breaded cheese pieces on the baking sheet, setting them about 1 inch apart.

4. Bake for about 3 minutes, or until the cheese is soft.

STORAGE: Leftover bites can be refrigerated in an airtight container for up to 2 days.

NOTES

Quinoa-Veggie Fritters

SUPERFOOD NUT-FREE GLUTEN-FREE VEGETARIAN

MAKES 10 FRITTERS
PREP TIME: 15 MINUTES • COOK TIME: 22 TO 25 MINUTES

Colorful, tasty, and surprisingly simple to prepare, these festive little fritters are sure to catch your busy toddler's eye. Cut them up into smaller pieces and present them along-side diced strawberries and kiwi for a real rainbow of a meal with an intriguing variety of textures and flavors. Serve them in a muffin tin for a fun presentation!

Variation: *Try replacing the zucchini with the same amount of diced broccoli or cauli-flower florets. These will give the fritters a chewier texture and sharper flavor. Keep in mind, however, that you'll have to sauté the broccoli or cauliflower for 3 to 4 minutes longer than the zucchini.*

1 tablespoon olive oil

⅔ cup diced zucchini

½ cup diced yellow onion

½ cup grated carrot

¼ cup fresh or frozen peas

1 large egg

1 cup grated cheddar or Monterey Jack
   cheese

1 cup cooked quinoa (see page 35)

1. Preheat the oven to 375°F. Line a 9-by-13-inch baking sheet with parchment paper.

2. In a medium sauté pan or skillet, heat the olive oil over medium heat.

3. Add the zucchini, onion, and carrot to the pan, and sauté for about 5 minutes.

4. Add the peas and cook for 2 to 5 minutes more. Allow to cool.

5. In a large bowl, whisk the egg and cheese together. Stir in the zucchini, onion, carrot, peas, and quinoa.

(Continued)

6. Using about ¼ cup of the mixture at a time, form patties with your hands and place them on the prepared baking sheet.

7. Bake for 10 minutes on one side, then flip and bake for 5 minutes more.

STORAGE: Leftover fritters can be refrigerated in an airtight container for up to 3 days or frozen for up to 3 months.

NOTES

Creamy Polenta with Tomato Sauce

NUT-FREE **GLUTEN-FREE** **VEGETARIAN**

MAKES 4 SERVINGS, ½ CUP EACH
PREP TIME: 5 MINUTES • COOK TIME: 10 MINUTES

Adaptable and easy to make, soft polenta has a texture similar to Cream of Wheat or grits. Polenta can also be baked—and even cut into shapes!—and works well in savory recipes, like this Italian-style favorite, as well as sweet dishes. Use canned or jarred tomato sauce to save time, or use your own homemade version, if you have some handy. Toddlers and grown-ups alike will ask for seconds!

Variation: *Pump up the nutritional value of your tomato sauce by adding a tablespoon of vegetable purée of your choice. Spinach, kale, and Swiss chard are good choices, as the acidity of the tomato sauce cuts the somewhat bitter taste of the leafy greens.*

4 cups water

1 cup quick-cooking polenta

2 tablespoons unsalted butter

½ cup cream cheese

¼ cup grated Parmesan cheese

2 tablespoons prepared tomato sauce

1. In a medium saucepan, bring the water to a boil over medium heat.

2. Slowly whisk in the polenta, stirring continuously for about 2 to 3 minutes or until it starts to thicken. Reduce the heat to maintain a simmer.

3. Whisk in the butter, cream cheese, and Parmesan, and continue to stir until the mixture has thickened, 3 to 5 minutes more.

4. Stir in the tomato sauce and cook until the sauce is warmed through, 1 to 2 minutes more.

   STORAGE: Leftover polenta can be refrigerated in an airtight container for up to 2 days.

   NOTES

Mexican "Pizza"

NUT-FREE **VEGETARIAN**

MAKES 2 SERVINGS

PREP TIME: 5 MINUTES • COOK TIME: 5 MINUTES

Pizza doesn't have to be the standard takeout variety. This Mexican-inspired adaptation doesn't even require sauce or dough, opting instead for beans and cheese on a whole-grain tortilla. With a couple of easy substitutions—corn tortillas for flour, and avocado for cheese—you'll have a gluten-free, dairy-free meal that's just as delicious. High in fiber, protein, and calcium, this no-fuss pizza could become a staple in your house.

Tip: *Instead of a knife, try using a pizza cutter to slice the pizza. Pizza cutters are also great for cutting pancakes and quesadillas. Just be sure to keep these sharp utensils far away from curious little fingers!*

½ cup canned vegetarian refried beans

1 large whole-grain tortilla

½ cup shredded cheddar or Monterey Jack cheese

1. Preheat the oven to 375°F. Line a 9-by-13-inch baking sheet with parchment paper or aluminum foil.

2. Spread the refried beans on the tortilla.

3. Sprinkle the cheese over the beans.

4. Place the tortilla on the prepared baking sheet. Bake for about 5 minutes or until the cheese has melted.

5. Cut the pizza into bite-size pieces before serving.

STORAGE: Leftover pizza can be refrigerated in an airtight container for up to 1 day.

NOTES ―――――――――――――――――――――――――――――

――――――――――――――――――――――――――――――――――

――――――――――――――――――――――――――――――――――

――――――――――――――――――――――――――――――――――

Mini Spinach Pizzas

SUPERFOOD · **NUT-FREE** · **VEGETARIAN**

MAKES 4 MINI PIZZAS
PREP TIME: 10 MINUTES • COOK TIME: 6 MINUTES

The combination of ricotta cheese and spinach on these pizzas packs a double dose of calcium, while the whole-wheat pita provides more fiber than regular pizza crust—and requires virtually no preparation! Fresh mozzarella balls, sometimes called bocconcini, also make an excellent toddler finger food on their own when chopped in half.

Variation: *The pitas in this recipe can be replaced with split whole-grain English muffins. Since English muffins are thicker and chewier, you might want to try cutting them into small squares before serving. Adding a tablespoon of marinara sauce before broiling will give extra flavor and help soften the English muffins.*

4 mini (3-inch) whole-wheat pitas, split

½ cup full-fat ricotta cheese

½ teaspoon dried oregano

1 (10-ounce) package frozen spinach, thawed and squeezed to remove excess moisture

½ pint fresh mozzarella balls (about 20 balls), halved

1. Heat the broiler, with the rack set about 4 inches from the heat source. Line a 9-by-13-inch baking sheet with aluminum foil.

2. Arrange the pita halves on the baking sheet with the cut side up.

3. In a small bowl, combine the ricotta cheese and oregano.

4. Spread the ricotta and oregano mixture on the pita halves, and top evenly with the spinach and mozzarella.

5. Broil until the cheese has melted and is starting to brown, 4 to 6 minutes.

STORAGE: These pizzas should be eaten immediately.

NOTES

Spinach Pesto Pasta

SUPERFOOD **NUT-FREE** **VEGETARIAN**

MAKES 4 SERVINGS, ½ CUP EACH
PREP TIME: 5 MINUTES • COOK TIME: 10 MINUTES

High in calcium, vitamin A, iron, and selenium, spinach deserves its reputation as a superfood, and this pesto packs plenty of it. It also skips the traditional addition of pine nuts, since some toddlers might not yet be ready to try nuts (pine nuts are a common allergen). Thanks to the basil and cheese, this pesto is flavorful enough that you won't miss them.

Variation: *If you do choose to add nuts to this recipe, try ½ cup toasted pine nuts (actually the edible seeds of pines) or raw walnuts. Both seeds and nuts are high in minerals and healthy fats and will add a rich, complex flavor to the pesto. If you have a family history of allergies, consult your pediatrician before introducing nuts or seeds to your toddler's diet.*

3 cups water

1 cup small-shape whole-wheat pasta
(such as ditalini or elbow macaroni)

2 cups baby spinach

1 cup chopped fresh basil

½ tablespoon freshly squeezed lemon juice

2 tablespoons grated Parmesan cheese

¼ cup olive oil

1. In a medium pot, bring the water to a boil over high heat.

2. Add the pasta and reduce the heat to medium. Cook until the pasta is tender, 5 to 8 minutes. Drain the pasta in a colander.

3. In a blender or food processor, combine the spinach, basil, lemon juice, Parmesan, and olive oil, and purée until smooth.

4. In a large bowl, combine the pasta and pesto.

STORAGE: Leftover pasta can be refrigerated in an airtight container for up to 2 days or frozen for up to 3 months.

NOTES

Speedy Pasta Primavera

SUPERFOOD | **NUT-FREE** | **VEGETARIAN**

MAKES 8 SERVINGS, ¼ CUP EACH
PREP TIME: 5 MINUTES • COOK TIME: 10 MINUTES

When you think of pasta primavera, chances are you imagine noodles accompanied by just a few julienned veggies drowning in a rich cream sauce. This recipe is heavier on the veggies than most and lighter on the cream; in fact, there's no cream involved—just a small amount of butter and Parmesan cheese for flavor. Plus, it's ready in minutes!

Variation: *For a wheat free version of this dish, try substituting brown rice pasta. Brown rice pasta is available in most of the same shapes as regular pasta and has a slightly firmer, chewier texture. It also takes slightly longer to cook, on average 12 to 15 minutes.*

3 cups water	½ cup shredded carrot
1 cup whole-wheat fusilli	½ cup chopped asparagus
1 tablespoon olive oil	1 tablespoon unsalted butter
½ cup shredded zucchini	2 tablespoons grated Parmesan cheese

1. In a large pot, bring the water to a boil over high heat. Add the pasta and reduce the heat to medium. Cook until the pasta is tender, about 10 minutes. Drain the pasta in a colander, reserving ¼ cup of the cooking water.

2. While the pasta is cooking, in a medium sauté pan or skillet, heat the olive oil over medium-high heat. Add the zucchini, carrot, and asparagus, and sauté until soft, about 8 minutes.

3. Transfer the vegetables to a large bowl. Combine the pasta, reserved pasta cooking water, zucchini, carrot, asparagus, butter, and Parmesan, and toss.

STORAGE: Leftover pasta can be refrigerated in an airtight container for up to 2 days.

NOTES

Gnocchi Bolognese

SUPERFOOD **NUT-FREE**

MAKES 8 SERVINGS, ½ CUP EACH
PREP TIME: 10 MINUTES • COOK TIME: 25 MINUTES

Italian for "dumplings," gnocchi are usually made with potatoes and cook faster than most pastas. They're soft, chewy, and fun to eat, and do a fine job of holding the hearty meat sauce in this recipe. A bonus to this tasty Bolognese: The grated carrot makes the sauce both sweeter and more nutritious, providing extra fiber and beta-carotene.

Variation: *Depending on the tolerance level of your toddler's taste buds and digestive system, you might want to liven up this Bolognese with a little onion and garlic. Add ⅓ cup diced yellow onion and 1 chopped garlic clove to the beef along with the carrots.*

1 tablespoon olive oil

1½ pounds ground beef

1 cup grated carrot

1 (14-ounce) can tomato purée

½ pound fresh or frozen gnocchi, cooked according to the package directions and drained

2 tablespoons grated Parmesan cheese

1. In a large saucepan, heat the olive oil over medium-high heat. Add the beef and cook, breaking it up with a spoon, until it begins to brown, about 4 minutes.

2. Add the carrot and cook until the meat is fully browned and the carrot is soft, about 5 minutes.

3. Add the tomato purée and bring to a simmer. Reduce the heat to medium.

4. Cook, stirring occasionally, until the liquid has reduced, about 15 minutes.

5. Serve over the cooked gnocchi and top with Parmesan cheese.

STORAGE: Leftover gnocchi can be refrigerated in an airtight container for up to 2 days.

NOTES _____

_____

_____

Baked Mini Rice Balls

SUPERFOOD **NUT-FREE** **VEGETARIAN**

MAKES 20 RICE BALLS

PREP TIME: 10 MINUTES • COOK TIME: 10 TO 16 MINUTES

An Italian delicacy beloved by adults and children alike, these balls are typically deep-fried but can be baked. This version is also more nutritious than the original because it uses brown rice in place of the traditional Arborio and features spinach. Chop these balls in half for young toddlers, or serve whole for older children with more teeth.

Variation: *These rice balls were made for dipping! Marinara sauce is a traditional, tasty choice, but Spinach Pesto (page 144) is just as delicious and doubles the leafy greens in this recipe. Or simply serve with a side of veggie purée.*

¼ cup whole-wheat pastry flour

2 large eggs, beaten

½ cup bread crumbs

1 cup cooked brown rice

⅓ cup shredded mozzarella cheese

¼ cup chopped spinach

1. Preheat the oven to 375°F. Line a 9-by-13-inch baking sheet with parchment paper.

2. Place the flour, beaten eggs, and bread crumbs in three separate small bowls.

3. In a medium bowl, combine the rice, cheese, and spinach.

4. Scoop up about 1 tablespoon of the mixture and roll it into a ball using your hands. Roll the ball in the flour, then dip it in the egg, and then roll it in the bread crumbs. Place the ball on the prepared baking sheet. Repeat with the remaining rice mixture.

5. Bake for 5 to 8 minutes; turn over and bake for 5 to 8 minutes more.

STORAGE: Leftover balls can be refrigerated in an airtight container for up to 3 days or frozen for up to 3 months.

NOTES _____

_____

_____

Chicken Fried Rice

SUPERFOOD DAIRY-FREE NUT-FREE GLUTEN-FREE

MAKES 4 SERVINGS, ¼ CUP EACH
PREP TIME: 5 MINUTES • COOK TIME: 15 MINUTES

Fresher and more nutritious than the Chinese takeout version, this healthy fried rice is even quicker to get on the table than delivery, thanks to the use of precooked rice and chicken. While the soy sauce or tamari gives this dish an authentic flavor, feel free to leave it out if you're concerned about sodium intake. If your toddler enjoys eating garlic, try adding a finely chopped clove of garlic while sautéing the veggies.

Variation: *If you're going for a more traditional fried rice with a chewier texture, substitute peas for the zucchini. Or for a meat-free version of this dish, skip the chicken and use both zucchini and peas (and any other veggies you like).*

½ tablespoon olive oil

1 small zucchini, diced

1 medium carrot, shredded

1 large egg, beaten

1 cup cooked brown rice

½ cup finely chopped cooked
   chicken breast

1 tablespoon low-sodium soy sauce or
   tamari (optional)

1. In medium skillet, heat the olive oil over medium-high heat.

2. Add the zucchini and carrot, and sauté until soft, about 8 minutes.

3. Pour the beaten egg over the vegetables, stirring while they cook.

4. Add the rice and chicken, and stir, mixing all the ingredients together.

5. Add the soy sauce, if desired, and stir again.

   STORAGE: Leftover rice can be refrigerated in an airtight container for up to 3 days.

   NOTES

Ham and Cheese Pockets

NUT-FREE

MAKES 9 POCKETS
PREP TIME: 10 MINUTES • COOK TIME: 15 MINUTES

Little ones love anything in "pocket" or turnover form, particularly the winning combination of ham and cheese. A lunchbox staple for decades, this recipe makes the combination more scrumptious by melting the cheese in a pizza crust, and more nutritious by adding broccoli florets. If your budget allows you to purchase organic ham, so much the better. Be sure to make extras for the rest of the family!

Variation: *Once you get the hang of making pockets with pizza dough, you can vary the fillings according to your preference or whatever you have in the refrigerator at the time. Try diced chicken with Monterey Jack cheese, peas, and carrots, or slice up meatballs and combine with mozzarella cheese and marinara sauce. The possibilities are endless!*

Cooking spray

¾ cup broccoli florets

1 cup diced deli ham

¾ cup shredded cheddar cheese

1 teaspoon dried parsley

3 tablespoons all-purpose flour

1 (12- to 14-ounce) package refrigerated whole-wheat pizza dough

2 tablespoons whole milk

1. Preheat the oven to 400°F. Line a 9-by-13-inch baking sheet with aluminum foil. Coat the foil with cooking spray.

2. In a medium bowl, combine the broccoli, ham, cheese, and parsley.

3. Dust a large cutting board with the flour. Unroll the pizza dough and place it on the board. Use a rolling pin to roll it into a 12-inch square. Cut it into 9 squares.

4. Spoon ¼ cup of the filling onto each square.

5. Using your fingers, moisten the edges of the dough with water, then fold the dough over, forming a triangle, to enclose the filling. Seal the edges with a fork, and prick a few holes in the top of each pocket.

(Continued)

6. Place the pockets on the prepared baking sheet, and brush each with a little milk.

7. Bake for 13 to 15 minutes, until golden brown.

   STORAGE: Leftover pockets can be refrigerated in an airtight container for up to 2 days or frozen for up to 3 months.

   NOTES

Fish Fingers

NUT-FREE

MAKES 8 FINGERS

PREP TIME: 5 MINUTES • COOK TIME: 15 MINUTES

White fish like the sole used in this recipe are mild in flavor and flaky in texture and make an appealing first taste of the sea. This easily digestible protein source is high in omega-3 fatty acids and vitamins D and B$_2$.

Tip: *Save half of the mayonnaise mixture for your little one to use as a dipping sauce; try mixing it with a squeeze of fresh lemon juice.*

¼ cup mayonnaise

1 teaspoon dried parsley

¼ teaspoon salt

1 cup bread crumbs

4 fresh sole fillets, cut into ½-inch-thick strips

Cooking spray

1. Preheat the oven to 425°F. Line a 9-by-13-inch baking sheet with parchment paper.

2. In a medium bowl, stir together the mayonnaise, parsley, and salt.

3. Place the bread crumbs in a shallow dish.

4. Gently roll the fish fingers in the mayonnaise mixture and then roll them in the bread crumbs to coat.

5. Place the coated fish on the prepared baking sheet and lightly spray them with cooking spray.

6. Bake for 12 to 15 minutes, or until the fish is flaky on the inside and golden brown on the outside.

STORAGE: Leftover fingers can be refrigerated in an airtight container for up to 2 days.

NOTES

Taco "Salad"

SUPERFOOD **NUT-FREE** **GLUTEN-FREE**

MAKES 8 SERVINGS, ¼ CUP EACH

PREP TIME: 5 MINUTES • COOK TIME: 10 MINUTES

No deep-fried tortilla bowl is needed for this easy-to-prepare Mexican meal. If your toddler has a taste for spices, try adding ½ teaspoon chili powder to this recipe when you mix the beef and beans; if not, the mixture is zesty enough on its own due to a bit of lime juice. Adults and older kids will like this served over a bed of shredded lettuce.

Variation: *Try topping this with shredded Monterey Jack or cheddar cheese. Canned or frozen corn kernels make a colorful addition, too, if you've introduced your toddler to corn with no problems.*

¾ cup lean ground beef

1 (15-ounce) can pinto beans, rinsed
  and drained

½ cup chopped avocado

½ cup diced fresh tomato

1 tablespoon freshly squeezed lime juice

1. In a large skillet, brown the beef over medium-high heat, breaking it into small pieces with a spoon and stirring continuously as it cooks, until cooked through. Drain the beef well and return it to the pan.

2. Mix in the beans and cook for 1 minute more.

3. Transfer the meat and bean mixture to a large bowl. Stir in the avocado and tomato. Top with the lime juice.

STORAGE: Leftover salad can be refrigerated in an airtight container for up to 1 day.

NOTES

Beef and Broccoli

SUPERFOOD · DAIRY-FREE · NUT-FREE · GLUTEN-FREE

PREP TIME: 5 MINUTES • COOK TIME: 13 MINUTES

Another healthy update of a Chinese takeout classic, this quickly cooked meal has all the iron, fiber, and flavor of the original without the added sodium and preservatives. Plus, making this at home means you can choose grass-fed or organic beef instead of the typical "mystery meat" so often sold at fast-food chains. This dish will win over even the most reluctant broccoli eater! Serve over rice, if desired, or with a side of noodles.

Tip: *The beef filet will cook more quickly (and be easier to chew) if it's been tenderized. Ask your butcher to do the work for you, or tenderize it yourself at home by placing the beef between two slices of wax paper and pounding it with a meat mallet for about 2 minutes.*

1 tablespoon olive oil

¾ pound filet of beef, cut into bite-size pieces

1 cup broccoli florets

½ cup water

1 tablespoon low sodium soy sauce (optional)

1 teaspoon sesame oil

1. In a large skillet, heat the olive oil over medium heat. Add the beef and cook, stirring occasionally, until browned, about 4 minutes. Transfer to a plate using a slotted spoon.

2. Add the broccoli and the water to the pan, and cook until the broccoli is tender and the liquid has evaporated, 5 to 8 minutes.

3. Return the beef and any collected juices to the pan, and cook, stirring, until the beef is warmed through, about 1 minute.

4. Remove from the heat. Add the soy sauce, if desired, and the sesame oil.

STORAGE: Leftover beef and broccoli can be refrigerated in an airtight container for up to 2 days.

NOTES

Good Greens Smoothie

SUPERFOOD **NUT-FREE** **GLUTEN-FREE** **VEGETARIAN**

MAKES 2 SERVINGS
PREP TIME: 10 MINUTES

Refreshing and sweet, this superfood smoothie lets kids drink their vegetables. Fresh spinach is a good choice when it comes to blending veggies in smoothie form, as it purées much more smoothly than other leafy greens. Using frozen rather than fresh berries will give this smoothie more of a milkshake consistency.

Variation: *Some kids don't like berries in smoothies because of the seeds. If that's the case with your little one, try substituting the same amount of papaya or banana, both of which make for super-smooth drinks.*

½ cup baby spinach

½ cup fresh or frozen mixed berries

½ cup full-fat plain yogurt

1 cup whole milk (soy or almond milk can be substituted)

In a blender or food processor, combine the spinach, berries, yogurt, and milk, and purée until smooth.

STORAGE: Smoothies should be consumed immediately.

NOTES ⎯⎯⎯⎯⎯⎯⎯⎯⎯⎯⎯⎯⎯⎯⎯⎯⎯⎯⎯⎯⎯⎯⎯⎯⎯⎯⎯

Strawberry-Banana Surprise Smoothie

GLUTEN-FREE **VEGETARIAN**

MAKES 2 SERVINGS

PREP TIME: 10 MINUTES

The "surprise" in this yummy drink is a little added protein in the form of your favorite nut or seed butter. Think of this as a frosty version of a PB&J that you can drink through a straw. Your toddler will slurp it up in no time.

Variation: *Fresh bananas and strawberries can be substituted for frozen; if you make this switch, add a few ice cubes to the blender. This is a good rule of thumb for smoothies in general: When using fresh fruit instead of frozen, the addition of ice cubes will make it more like a milkshake.*

½ cup frozen banana slices

½ cup frozen strawberries

1 tablespoon peanut, almond, cashew, or sunflower seed butter

½ cup full-fat plain yogurt

1 cup whole milk (soy or almond milk can be substituted)

In a blender or food processor, combine the banana, strawberries, peanut butter, yogurt, and milk, and purée until smooth.

STORAGE: Smoothies should be consumed immediately.

NOTES

Almond Butter Cereal Balls

GLUTEN-FREE VEGETARIAN

MAKES ABOUT 12 BALLS

PREP TIME: 5 MINUTES • COOK TIME: 1 TO 2 MINUTES
PLUS 15 MINUTES REFRIGERATION TIME

Better than a batch of oatmeal cookies, these sweet cereal balls are filled with wholesome ingredients. Almond butter, for example, is high in calcium, protein, magnesium, and vitamin E; rolled oats add fiber. The brown rice cereal imparts a satisfying crunch.

⅓ cup agave nectar or honey (for babies over 12 months only)

¼ cup almond butter

2 tablespoons unsalted butter

1 cup crispy brown rice cereal

1 cup old-fashioned rolled oats

¼ cup raisins

1. Line a 9-by-13-inch baking sheet with parchment paper.

2. In a small saucepan, combine the agave nectar, almond butter, and butter and cook over medium heat, stirring occasionally, for 1 to 2 minutes.

3. Remove the pan from the heat and stir in the cereal, oats, and raisins.

4. Drop the mixture by tablespoons onto the baking sheet.

5. Refrigerate for 15 minutes before serving.

STORAGE: Leftover cereal balls can be refrigerated in an airtight container for up to 1 week.

NOTES

Sunflower Seed Butter and Banana Pinwheels

SUPERFOOD **NUT-FREE** **VEGETARIAN** VEGAN

MAKES ABOUT 8 PINWHEELS
PREP TIME: 10 MINUTES

Less allergenic than nut butters, sunflower seed butter boasts the same creamy texture as peanut butter and provides vitamin E, protein, magnesium, and selenium. Use it as a replacement in the classic PB&J (now off-limits in many school cafeterias and class-rooms), cookies, or anywhere else you might use peanut butter, like these pinwheels.

Variation: *If your toddler doesn't have nut allergies, almond butter or cashew butter can be substituted for the sunflower seed butter. Almond butter is slightly creamier than cashew butter, but the latter is generally sweeter. Both will make you wonder why you've been in a peanut butter rut for so long!*

1 tablespoon sunflower seed butter

⅛ cup banana slices

1 small whole-wheat tortilla

1. Spread the sunflower seed butter over the tortilla.

2. Place the banana slices over the sunflower seed butter, leaving the edges on one side uncovered.

3. Starting on the banana-covered side, roll up the tortilla into a tight cylinder. Cut crosswise into pinwheels.

STORAGE: Leftover pinwheels can be refrigerated in an airtight container for up to 1 day.

NOTES

Zucchini Mini Muffins

DAIRY-FREE **NUT-FREE** **VEGETARIAN**

MAKES ABOUT 24 MINI MUFFINS

PREP TIME: 5 MINUTES • COOK TIME: 15 MINUTES

A natural sweetener derived from the agave plant, agave nectar won't cause a blood sugar spike the way most sweets do. If you'd prefer not to use sweetener, replace agave nectar with the same amount of banana or apple purée.

Variation: *Try substituting the same amount of shredded carrots for the zucchini, or use a mixture of both.*

⅓ cup plus 2 teaspoons olive oil

Cooking spray (optional)

2 cups whole-wheat pastry flour

½ teaspoon baking soda

2 teaspoons baking powder

½ teaspoon salt

2 large eggs, beaten

⅔ cup agave nectar

1½ cups shredded zucchini

1. Preheat the oven to 350°F. Grease the wells of a standard mini muffin tin with 2 teaspoons of the olive oil, or spray them with cooking spray.

2. In a large bowl, combine the flour, baking soda, baking powder, and salt.

3. In a small bowl, stir together the remaining ⅓ cup olive oil, the agave nectar, and the zucchini.

4. Pour the wet ingredients into the bowl with the dry ingredients and stir until just mixed.

5. Pour the batter into the muffin tin until each well is about ⅔ full.

6. Bake for 15 minutes.

STORAGE: Leftover muffins can be refrigerated in an airtight container for up to 1 week or frozen for up to 3 months.

NOTES _____

_____

Edamame Hummus

DAIRY-FREE **NUT-FREE** GLUTEN-FREE VEGAN

MAKES 6 SERVINGS, ¼ CUP EACH
PREP TIME: 5 MINUTES • COOK TIME: 3 MINUTES

Edamame, or green soybeans, are super high in fiber and protein, and make a great snack for older kids and adults when the edamame are still in the pods (which are inedible). For toddlers, edamame can be served shelled as a finger food or blended into a hummus like this one with tahini (sesame seed paste), which adds calcium, vitamin E, and magnesium. Serve with mini whole-wheat pitas and steamed veggies, or try it in Hummus and Carrot Pinwheels (page 162).

Tip: *Add the olive oil after the other ingredients are mostly mixed together, as it blends more quickly than the chunky edamame and thick, sticky tahini. Pour the oil in slowly, if possible, to ensure a more even distribution.*

3 cups water

1 cup frozen shelled edamame

¼ cup tahini

1 tablespoon freshly squeezed lemon juice

1 tablespoon olive oil

1. In a medium pot, bring the water to a boil over medium heat.

2. Add the edamame and cook for 2 to 3 minutes. Drain the edamame in a colander and allow to cool.

3. In a blender or food processor, combine the edamame, tahini, lemon juice, and oil, and blend until smooth.

   STORAGE: Leftover hummus can be refrigerated in an airtight container for up to 1 week.

   NOTES

White Bean Dip

DAIRY-FREE **NUT-FREE** GLUTEN-FREE VEGAN

MAKES 6 SERVINGS, ¼ CUP EACH
PREP TIME: 10 MINUTES

Similar to hummus but smoother in texture, white bean dip (made with cannellini beans) is equally high in protein and fiber. This dip pairs well with steamed vegetable chunks or soft pieces of bread or pita for dipping; it also makes an excellent vegetarian sandwich spread for adults.

Variation: *Fresh herbs such as thyme, tarragon, or marjoram make a tasty addition to this dip; use about ¼ teaspoon of any of these. Thyme will give the dip a slightly Italian flavor, while tarragon and marjoram will make it sweeter and more fragrant.*

1 (16-ounce) can cannellini beans, drained and rinsed

2 tablespoons freshly squeezed lemon juice

¼ cup tahini

2 tablespoons olive oil

In a blender or food processor, combine the beans, lemon juice, tahini, and olive oil, and blend until smooth.

STORAGE: Leftover white bean dip can be refrigerated in an airtight container for up to 1 week.

NOTES _____

_____

_____

_____

Cheese Fondue Dip

NUT-FREE **VEGETARIAN**

MAKES 4 SERVINGS, ¼ CUP EACH
PREP TIME: 5 MINUTES • COOK TIME: 10 MINUTES

Kids will eat almost anything covered or dipped in cheese. Unlike most varieties of cheese sauces, which are highly processed, this one won't make you feel guilty about smothering your tot's veggies. It goes particularly well with steamed broccoli or cauliflower florets, cooked carrots, green beans, and asparagus.

Tip: *All-purpose flour is recommended for this recipe instead of whole-wheat pastry flour because of its extremely mild taste (and the small amount used). If your toddler is allergic to wheat, brown rice flour can be substituted.*

2 tablespoons unsalted butter

2 tablespoons all-purpose flour

1 cup whole milk

1 cup grated cheddar or Monterey Jack cheese

1. In a medium saucepan, melt the butter over medium-low heat.

2. Once the butter has melted, add the flour little by little, whisking to prevent lumps.

3. Reduce the heat to low and cook for about 3 minutes, but don't allow the mixture to brown.

4. Remove the pan from the heat and slowly whisk in the milk.

5. Return the milk mixture to the stovetop over medium heat and cook for about 5 minutes, until the sauce is thick enough to coat the back of a spoon.

6. Add the cheese and stir until it has melted completely.

STORAGE: Leftover cheese dip can be refrigerated in an airtight container for up to 3 days.

NOTES

Hummus and Carrot Pinwheels

SUPERFOOD   NUT-FREE   VEGAN

MAKES ABOUT 8 PINWHEELS
PREP TIME: 10 MINUTES

Fun to look at and fun to eat, pinwheels are a clever way to hide veggies in your little one's snack. They also make a nifty lunch when you're on the go—just be sure to pack them in an insulated bag with an ice pack so they stay fresh. Other grated veggies, such as cucumbers and beets, work well in these pinwheels in place of carrots; you can also try tossing in a few baby spinach leaves.

Variation: *For extra color, swap out the whole-wheat tortilla for a spinach- or red pepper–flavored kind. You can also replace the hummus with cream cheese.*

1 tablespoon hummus

1 tablespoon shredded carrot

1 small whole-wheat tortilla

1. Spread the hummus over the tortilla.

2. Sprinkle the carrot over the hummus, leaving the edges on one side uncovered.

3. Starting on the carrot-covered side, roll up the tortilla into a tight cylinder. Cut the roll crosswise into pinwheels.

   STORAGE: Leftover pinwheels can be refrigerated in an airtight container for up to 1 day.

   NOTES

Cheesy Carrot Balls

SUPERFOOD   **NUT-FREE**   **GLUTEN-FREE**   **VEGETARIAN**

MAKES ABOUT 12 BALLS
PREP TIME: 5 MINUTES

Reminiscent of the larger cheese balls often served as appetizers at parties, these smaller spheres are more nutritious, thanks to the carrots, but just as delicious. Kids love the squishy texture—plus, they're super easy to chew. These can also be spread between slices of bread or in a pita.

Variation: *Mixing in a tablespoon of wheat germ or ground flax meal will help hold these balls together and add more fiber and vitamin E. Or for a fruit-and-cheese platter type of flavor, try replacing the grated carrot with the same amount of grated apple.*

½ cup cold cream cheese

1 cup grated cheddar cheese

½ cup finely grated carrot

1. In a medium bowl, combine the cream cheese, cheddar, and carrot.

2. Scoop up about 1 tablespoon of the mixture and, using wet hands, gently form the mixture into a ball. Repeat until all of the mixture has been used.

   STORAGE: Leftover cheese balls can be refrigerated in an airtight container for up to 2 days.

   NOTES ————————————————————————————

Recipes for the One-Year Birthday Party

• • • • • • • • • • • • • • • • • • • •

Congratulations! Your baby's first birthday is one of the most exciting, monumental occasions of his life—and yours. And after 12 months of many sleepless nights, laughs, tears, milestones, and messes, your entire family deserves a celebration.

The recipes in this section are meant to be fun and easy crowd-pleasers for all ages. Remember, your baby is still too young to appreciate the difference between a culinary work of art and a humble pie (or cake, as the case may be), and so are most of the young guests in attendance. Cut yourself some slack and enjoy this most wonderful day.

Coconut-Pineapple Ice Pops

DAIRY-FREE GLUTEN-FREE **NUT-FREE** VEGAN

MAKES ABOUT 8–10 POPS

PREP TIME: 15 MINUTES, PLUS 6 HOURS TO FREEZE

Creamy coconut milk and sweet pineapple make these tropical ice pops irresistible. Freeze them in ice pop molds or use paper cups. Cover the cups with foil, and then insert the ice pop stick through the foil into the fruit mixture. The foil will hold the sticks in place while the ice pops freeze.

3 cups pineapple, cut into small pieces   ½ cup coconut milk (full fat)

⅔ cup sugar

1. In a food processor or blender, combine the pineapple, sugar, and coconut milk, and process until well combined, 30 seconds to 1 minute.

2. Pour the mixture through a fine-mesh sieve into a liquid measuring cup.

3. Pour the strained mixture into ice pop molds.

4. Freeze the ice pops until frozen, about 6 hours, before serving.

STORAGE: Remaining ice pops can be stored in the freezer for up to 3 months.

NOTES

Banana-Blueberry Cake
with Cream Cheese Frosting

NUT-FREE VEGETARIAN

MAKES 4 TO 6 SERVINGS

PREP TIME: 20 MINUTES • COOK TIME: 20 MINUTES

This cake is low in sugar and contains healthy bananas, making it the ideal cake for a first birthday party. Your toddler is already very familiar with the flavor of bananas, so he'll love this sweet cake, which is guaranteed to be a crowd pleaser. Use very ripe bananas for best results. Decorate the top of the cake with mini chocolate chips or some other fun and festive topping.

FOR THE CAKE:

1½ cups whole-wheat flour

1 teaspoon baking soda

1 teaspoon ground cinnamon

¼ teaspoon ground nutmeg

Pinch of salt

4 ripe bananas

¾ cup unsweetened applesauce

1 teaspoon vanilla extract

2 egg whites, beaten

1 cup blueberries

FOR THE FROSTING:

8 ounces cream cheese, softened

¼ cup unsweetened applesauce

½ teaspoon vanilla extract

To make the cake:

1. Preheat the oven to 400°F.

2. Grease and flour two 9-inch round cake pans.

3. In a large bowl, whisk together the flour, baking soda, cinnamon, nutmeg, and salt.

4. In a separate large bowl, mash together the bananas and applesauce. Stir in the vanilla extract and beaten egg whites.

5. Fold the wet ingredients into the dry ingredients until they are just incorporated. Fold in the blueberries.

6. Pour the batter into the prepared cake pans, and bake them until a toothpick inserted in the center comes out clean, about 20 minutes.

7. Cool the cakes on a wire rack.

To make the frosting:

1. In a medium bowl, mix together the cream cheese, applesauce, and vanilla extract.

2. Turn one cake out onto a cake plate, and spread it with half the frosting.

3. Turn the second cake out on top of the first cake, and spread it with the remaining frosting.

4. Store in a box or covered cake stand until the moment of presentation.

STORAGE: Leftover birthday cake can be refrigerated in an airtight container for up to 3 days, or frozen for up to 3 months.

NOTES

Strawberry Cream Hearts

NUT-FREE **VEGETARIAN**

MAKES ABOUT 18 HEARTS
PREP TIME: 10 MINUTES • COOK TIME: 10 MINUTES

These gorgeous little puffs look like an expert pastry chef spent hours creating them, but they're actually incredibly simple to make. Fresh raspberries can be used in place of the strawberries if your toddler prefers them, or try using a combination of both.

1 cup heavy cream

1 teaspoon pure vanilla extract

¼ cup confectioners' sugar

1 package frozen puff pastry, defrosted

½ cup sliced fresh strawberries

1. Preheat the oven to 400°F. Line a 9-by-13-inch baking sheet with parchment paper.

2. In the bowl of a stand mixer fitted with the paddle attachment, combine the cream, vanilla, and sugar and beat until fluffy, about 5 minutes.

3. Unfold the puff pastry and cut it into hearts using a heart-shaped cookie cutter.

4. Place the hearts on the baking sheet and bake until golden brown, about 10 minutes.

5. Allow the hearts to cool, then cut them in half crosswise to make two hearts. Top one half with whipped cream and berries, then place the other half on top to form a sandwich.

STORAGE: Leftover hearts can be refrigerated in an airtight container for up to 1 day.

NOTES _____

_____

_____

_____

Watermelon "Cookies"

DAIRY-FREE   GLUTEN-FREE   **NUT-FREE**   VEGAN

MAKES ABOUT 24 COOKIES
PREP TIME: 5 MINUTES

Probably the simplest dessert you'll ever make, these one-ingredient "cookies" are ideal for summer birthdays. Just be sure to use a seedless watermelon, as toddlers generally aren't skilled at spitting out seeds. Try to find a firm melon—mushy melon won't hold the shape of the cookie cutter as well.

1 small seedless watermelon

1. Cut the watermelon into ½-inch-thick slices.

2. Use cookie cutters in a variety of shapes (stars, letters, numbers, hearts) to cut the watermelon slices into "cookies."

STORAGE: Leftover watermelon cookies can be refrigerated in an airtight container for up to 2 days.

NOTES

Chocolate Chip Cookie Pie

NUT-FREE **VEGETARIAN**

MAKES ABOUT 12 SERVINGS
PREP TIME: 10 MINUTES • COOK TIME: 20 MINUTES

With a chocolate chip cookie that's so big and dense it's really a pie, you can expect your guests to line up for seconds . . . and maybe even thirds! This pie is best if you don't let it bake for too long, so be sure to take it out of the oven as soon as it's golden brown all over and a toothpick stuck into the middle comes out clean.

½ cup unsalted butter, at room temperature, plus more for the pan

½ cup packed brown sugar

¼ cup granulated sugar

1 large egg

2 teaspoons pure vanilla extract

1 cup whole-wheat pastry flour

½ teaspoon baking powder

¼ teaspoon salt

1 cup semisweet chocolate chips

1. Preheat the oven to 375°F. Butter a 9-inch pie plate.

2. In the bowl of a stand mixer fitted with the paddle attachment, beat the butter, brown sugar, and granulated sugar until fluffy, about 5 minutes.

3. Add the egg and vanilla, and beat for 2 minutes more. Remove the bowl from the mixer.

4. In a separate large bowl, mix the flour, baking powder, and salt. Slowly stir the dry ingredients into the bowl with the wet ingredients.

5. Stir in the chocolate chips.

6. Press the dough into the prepared pie plate, and bake for 20 minutes, or until golden brown.

STORAGE: Leftover pie can be stored at room temperature in an airtight container for up to 3 days.

NOTES

RECIPES FOR THE ONE-YEAR BIRTHDAY PARTY

Sample Meal Plans

On the following pages, you'll find sample meal plans for the various ages using recipes from this book, as well as simple snack suggestions that require almost no preparation. Simple suggestions that do not require recipes will have two asterisks (**) next to them. Keep in mind that all meals should be supplemented by liquids, whether that's breast milk or formula in the first 12 months, or cow's milk, almond milk, soy milk, or other liquids after that point. Refer back to the recipe chapters for specifics on how much of these liquids should be consumed at each age.

4 TO 6 MONTHS

When your baby first begins solids, try offering just one purée each day, keeping in mind the 4-day wait rule before introducing new foods. Once a couple of foods have been introduced without a reaction, feel free to mix purées for more variety.

After a couple of weeks of doing well with just one purée, you can start offering purées a couple of times each day.

WEEK	MONDAY	TUESDAY	WEDNESDAY	THURSDAY	FRIDAY	SATURDAY	SUNDAY
1	· Sweet Potato Purée	· Sweet Potato Purée	· Sweet Potato Purée	· Sweet Potato Purée	· Green Bean Purée	· Green Bean Purée	· Green Bean Purée
2	· Green Bean Purée	· Apple Purée	· Apple Purée	· Apple Purée	· Apple Purée	· Brown Rice Cereal	· Brown Rice Cereal
3	· Brown Rice Cereal · Apple Purée	· Brown Rice Cereal · Sweet Potato and Green Beans Purée	· Green Bean Purée · Mashed Avocado	· Apple Purée · Mashed Avocado	· Sweet Potato Purée · Mashed Avocado	· Brown Rice Cereal · Mashed Avocado	· Sweet Potato Purée · Green Bean Purée
4	· Brown Rice Cereal · Mashed Banana	· Green Bean Purée · Mashed Banana	· Sweet Potato and Apple Purée · Mashed Banana	· Apple Purée · Avocado and Banana Purée	· Brown Rice Cereal · Carrot Purée	· Sweet Potato and Green Beans Purée · Carrot Purée	· Mashed Banana · Carrot Purée

7 TO 8 MONTHS

Babies move at different rates when it comes to all things, but especially in the case of food. Whether you started foods at 4 months or 6 months, your baby's reactions to food will tell you what she's capable of handling, and whether she wants more. By 7 to 8 months, some babies will still treat purées with cautious skepticism, while others will be ready to move to three feedings a day. Here is a sample month that begins with two purées a day and progresses to three each day after the first couple of weeks. Adapt as feels appropriate with your particular child, and continue to follow the breast milk or formula recommendations noted in chapter 4.

WEEK	MONDAY	TUESDAY	WEDNESDAY	THURSDAY	FRIDAY	SATURDAY	SUNDAY
1	· Avocado, Sweet Potato, and Brown Rice Purée · Carrot Purée	· Cauliflower and Sweet Potato Purée · Quinoa and Banana Purée	· Cauliflower and Carrot Purée · Mashed Avocado	· Cauliflower Purée · Apple Pie Oatmeal Purée	· Blueberries and Quinoa Purée · Cauliflower and Sweet Potato Purée	· Blueberry-Apple Yogurt Purée · Quinoa and Banana Purée	· Blueberry Purée · Avocado, Sweet Potato, and Brown Rice Purée
2	· Butternut Squash, Cauliflower, and Peas Purée · Blueberries and Quinoa Purée	· Peach, Blueberries, and Carrot Purée · Quinoa and Banana Purée	· Avocado, Sweet Potato, and Brown Rice Purée · Peach Purée	· Apple Pie Oatmeal Purée · Peach, Blueberries, and Carrot Purée	· Cauliflower and Sweet Potato Purée · Peach and Carrot Purée	· Broccoli, Cauliflower, and Carrot Purée · Brown Rice Cereal	· Peas, Pear, and Broccoli Purée · Blueberries and Quinoa Purée
3	· Broccoli Purée · Avocado and Pear Purée · Brown Rice Cereal	· Broccoli, Cauliflower, and Carrot Purée · Peas and Carrots Purée · Apple and Banana Purée	· Green Bean and Sweet Potato Purée · Chicken, Pears, and Quinoa Purée · Peach, Blueberries, and Carrot Purée	· Chicken and Avocado Purée · Zucchini and Banana Purée · Blueberries and Quinoa Purée	· Quinoa and Banana Purée · Chicken and Zucchini Purée · Broccoli, Cauliflower, and Carrot Purée	· Chicken, Pears, and Quinoa Purée · Zucchini Purée · Peach, Blueberries, and Carrot Purée	· Zucchini and Banana Purée · Blueberry-Apple Yogurt Purée · Pork, Carrots, and Brown Rice Purée
4	· Pork and Apples Purée · Quinoa and Banana Purée · Cauliflower and Sweet Potato Purée	· Pork, Carrots, and Brown Rice Purée · Blueberry-Apple Yogurt Purée · Sweet Potato and Green Beans Purée	· Pork and Apples Purée · Peas, Pear, and Broccoli Purée · Avocado, Sweet Potato, and Brown Rice Purée	· Broccoli, Cauliflower, and Carrot Purée · Carrot and Mango Purée · Chicken, Pears, and Quinoa Purée	· Blueberries and Quinoa Purée · Apple and Mango Purée · Sweet Potato and Green Beans Purée	· Pork, Carrots, and Brown Rice Purée · Mango Purée · Cauliflower and Sweet Potato Purée	· Carrot and Mango Purée · Chicken and Zucchini Purée · Blueberries and Quinoa Purée

SAMPLE MEAL PLANS

9 TO 11 MONTHS

Your baby is really eating now! The one-week plan presented here includes a couple of complementary recipes for breakfast, lunch, and dinner so your baby gets a full, nutritionally balanced meal. Some babies will eat up both options; others might prefer to eat just one. Follow your baby's cues. Experiment with blending purées to different textures to find out what your baby likes and may be ready for.

By this point, you can start to supplement purées with finger foods and snacks one or two times a day. Keep snacks simple. It's exciting when your baby begins to self-feed, but messy too! As with previous months, breast milk or formula remains incredibly important for your baby's health and nutrition. Follow recommendations noted in chapter 5.

	MONDAY	TUESDAY	WEDNESDAY	THURSDAY	FRIDAY	SATURDAY	SUNDAY
Breakfast	· Avocado, Sweet Potato, and Brown Rice Purée · Papaya, Banana, and Cantaloupe Yogurt Purée	· Blueberry-Apple Yogurt Purée · Brown Rice Cereal · Mashed Mango	· Peach, Plum, and Strawberry Oatmeal Purée · Cottage cheese**	· Cottage Cheese and Kiwi · Apple Pie Oatmeal Purée	· Blueberries and Quinoa Purée · Puréed cantaloupe · Cooked egg**	· Applesauce Muffins · Cheese chunks** · Sliced banana**	· Blueberries and Quinoa Purée · Cottage cheese** · Mashed cooked carrot**
Lunch	· Chickpea, Sweet Potato, and Cauliflower Purée · Apple and Mango Purée	· Tasty Turkey, Sweet Potato and Bean Stew · Apple Purée with Cottage Cheese	· Tofu, Quinoa, and Avocado Bowl · Peas and Carrots Purée	· Leftover Chicken and Brown Rice with Sautéed Kale · Sweet Potato and Green Beans Purée	· Beef and Parsnips Purée	· Mini Meat Loaf Muffins · Broccoli, Cauliflower, and Carrot Purée · Baked Pear Slices	· Chicken, Peach, and Pumpkin Purée · Brown rice · Green Bean Purée
Dinner	· Tasty Turkey, Sweet Potato and Bean Stew · Blueberry-Apple Yogurt Purée	· Tofu, Quinoa, and Avocado Bowl · Broccoli, Cauliflower, and Carrot Purée	· Butternut Squash "Mac and Cheese" · Peas, Pear, and Broccoli Purée	· Beef and Parsnips Purée · Kiwi, Asparagus, and Banana Purée	· Mini Meat Loaf Muffins · Broccoli, Cauliflower, and Carrot Purée · Puréed Apricot	· Chicken, Peach, and Pumpkin Purée · Brown rice**	· Tofu, Quinoa, and Avocado Bowl · Peach, Blueberries, and Carrot Purée
Snacks	· Whole grain toast strips or soft crackers** · Sliced pear**	· Banana slices** · Steamed green beans**	· Roasted Sweet Potato Nibbles · Cooked minced chicken**	· Banana slices** · Apple purée mixed with yogurt	· Whole grain cracker** · Mashed nectarine** · Applesauce Muffins	· Tofu Bites · Avocado Toast · Yogurt**	· Cottage cheese**

12 TO 18 MONTHS

It's almost like children have a sixth sense when it comes to parent desperation, and particularly so in the case of food. The more we want them to eat healthily and heartily, the better an idea it seems to them to refuse food. As you've no doubt learned over the course of the last several months, babies will make their own decisions about what they will and won't eat (just as we do). At this point, the good news is that you and your baby can largely enjoy the same meals, so whatever she doesn't eat, feel free to put it away yourself.

Babies are amazing managers of their own food intake. In the 12- to 18-month range, it's common for some to eat a big lunch and go very light on dinner, or vice versa. Your baby's variable eating habits should not necessarily be a cause for concern, but always consult your pediatrician if you're worried. Now that you can start to introduce cow's milk and honey in your baby's diet, virtually nothing is off the table.

	MONDAY	TUESDAY	WEDNESDAY	THURSDAY	FRIDAY	SATURDAY	SUNDAY
Breakfast	• Whole-Wheat Banana Pancakes • Strawberry Purée • Cheese slices**	• Peach, Plum, and Strawberry Oatmeal	• Breakfast Couscous • Yogurt with mashed blueberries**	• Scrambled eggs** • Whole wheat toast strips** • Cottage Cheese and Kiwi	• Tofu Scramble with shredded cheese • ½ English muffin** • Orange segments**	• Blueberry and Quinoa Purée • Yogurt**	• Toasted whole grain fingers with cream cheese** • ½ hard-boiled egg, chopped** • Melon slices**
Lunch	• Ham and Cheese Pockets • Apple and Mango Purée	• Chicken Fried Rice • Red pepper strips** • Banana slices**	• Quick Red Lentil Soup • ¼ whole wheat pita** • Melon slices**	• Fish Fingers • Confetti Couscous • Red pepper slices**	• Beef and Broccoli • Quinoa (cooked) • Raspberries**	• Mini Apple Turkey Meatballs • Quinoa (cooked) • Tomato slices**	• Butternut Squash "Mac and Cheese" • Cucumber sticks** • Red pepper sticks**
Dinner	• Chicken Fried Rice • Steamed broccoli florets** • Applesauce (Apple Purée)	• Taco "Salad" • Shredded cheese** • ½ whole grain tortilla**	• Fish Fingers • Speedy Pasta Primavera	• Beef and Broccoli • Brown rice** • Sliced banana and papaya**	• Mini Apple Turkey Meatballs • Confetti Couscous • Sliced plums**	• Mini Spinach Pizzas with chopped chicken • Cottage cheese** • Roasted Sweet Potato Nibbles	• Leftover Chicken and Brown Rice with Sautéed Kale • Steamed turnip and carrots** • Apple Purée
Snacks	• Cucumber sticks** • Peach slices (ripe)** • Hummus and Carrot Pinwheels • Yogurt**	• Cheesy Carrot Balls • Mango slices**	• Pear slices** • Cheesy Carrot Balls	• Yogurt** • Roasted Sweet Potato Nibbles	• Good Greens Smoothie • Yogurt**	• Apple slices with sunflower butter** • Strawberry Banana Surprise Smoothie	• Cheese slices** • Zucchini Mini Muffins

SAMPLE MEAL PLANS

Measurement Conversions

● ● ● ● ● ● ● ● ● ● ● ● ● ● ● ● ● ● ●

VOLUME EQUIVALENTS (LIQUID)

US STANDARD	US STANDARD (OUNCES)	METRIC (APPROXIMATE)
2 tablespoons	1 fl. oz.	30 mL
¼ cup	2 fl. oz.	60 mL
½ cup	4 fl. oz.	120 mL
1 cup	8 fl. oz.	240 mL
1½ cups	12 fl. oz.	355 mL
2 cups or 1 pint	16 fl. oz.	475 mL
4 cups or 1 quart	32 fl. oz.	1 L
1 gallon	128 fl. oz.	4 L

OVEN TEMPERATURES

FAHRENHEIT (F)	CELSIUS (C) (APPROXIMATE)
250	120
300	150
325	165
350	180
375	190
400	200
425	220
450	230

VOLUME EQUIVALENTS (DRY)

US STANDARD	METRIC (APPROXIMATE)
⅛ teaspoon	0.5 mL
¼ teaspoon	1 mL
½ teaspoon	2 mL
¾ teaspoon	4 mL
1 teaspoon	5 mL
1 tablespoon	15 mL
¼ cup	59 mL
⅓ cup	79 mL
½ cup	118 mL
⅔ cup	156 mL
¾ cup	177 mL
1 cup	235 mL
2 cups or 1 pint	475 mL
3 cups	700 mL
4 cups or 1 quart	1 L

WEIGHT EQUIVALENTS

US STANDARD	METRIC (APPROXIMATE)
½ ounce	15 g
1 ounce	30 g
2 ounces	60 g
4 ounces	115 g
8 ounces	225 g
12 ounces	340 g
16 ounces or 1 pound	455 g

References

American Academy of Asthma, Allergy and Immunology. "Preventing Allergies: What You Should Know About Your Baby's Nutrition." Accessed June 14, 2014. http://www.aaaai.org/conditions -and-treatments/library/at-a-glance /prevention-of-allergies-and-asthma- in-children.aspx.

American Academy of Environmental Medicine. "Genetically Modified Foods." Accessed June 14, 2014. http://www .aaemonline.org/gmopost.html.

American Academy of Pediatrics. "AAP Reaffirms Breastfeeding Guidelines." February 27, 2012. Accessed June 16, 2014. http://www.aap.org/en-us/about-the-aap /aap-press-room/Pages/AAP-Reaffirms -Breastfeeding-Guidelines.aspx.

American Academy of Pediatrics. "AAP Makes Recommendations to Reduce Children's Exposure to Pesticides." Accessed June 13, 2014. http://www.aap .org/en-us/about-the-aap/aap-press-room /Pages/AAP-Makes-Recommendations -to-Reduce-Children's-Exposure-to -Pesticides.aspx.

American Academy of Pediatrics. "Infant Food and Feeding." Accessed June 15, 2014. http://www.aap.org/en-us /advocacy-and-policy/aap-health -initiatives/HALF-Implementation -Guide/Age-Specific-Content/Pages /Infant-Food-and-Feeding.aspx.

American Academy of Pediatrics. "The Use of Cow's Milk in Infancy." 1992. Accessed June 15, 2014. http://pediatrics .aappublications.org/content/89/6/1105.

American Dietetic Association Complete Food and Nutrition Guide. 4th ed. Hoboken, N.J.: John Wiley and Sons, 2012.

American Dietetic Association. "Fresh, Canned, or Frozen—Get the Most from Your Fruits and Vegetables." Accessed June 14, 2014. http://www.eatright.org /Public/content.aspx?id=6442451032.

American Heart Association. "Fish and Omega-3 Fatty Acids." Accessed June 15, 2014. http://www.heart.org/HEARTORG /General/Fish-and-Omega-3-Fatty-Acids _UCM_303248_Article.jsp.

Centers for Disease Control and Prevention. "Food Allergies in Schools." Accessed June 14, 2014. http://www.cdc.gov /healthyyouth/foodallergies.

Centers for Disease Control and Prevention. "Listeria and Food." Accessed June 15, 2014. http://www.cdc.gov/foodsafety /specific-foods/listeria-and-food.html.

The Environmental Working Group. "EWG's 2014 Shopper's Guide to Pesticides in Produce." April 2014. Accessed June 14, 2014. http://www.ewg.org/foodnews /summary.php.

Epstein, Samuel S. "American Public Health Association: Ban Genetically Engineered Hormonal rBGH Milk, Meat Adulterated With Sex Hormones." *The Huffington Post.* Accessed June 14, 2014. http://www .huffingtonpost.com/samuel-s-epstein /american-public-health-a_b_399147.html.

Fleischer, David M., MD. "Early Introduction of Allergenic Foods May Prevent Food Allergy in Children." *American Academy of Pediatrics News.* February 2013. Accessed June 15, 2014. http://aapnewsde.aap.org /aapnews-open/201302_0?pg=13#pg13.

Greer, Frank R., MD, Scott H. Sicherer, MD, A. Wesley Burks, MD, and the Committee on Nutrition and Section on Allergy and Immunology. "Effects of Early Nutritional Interventions on the Development of Atopic Disease in Infants and Children: The Role of Maternal Dietary Restriction, Breastfeeding, Timing of Introduction of Complementary Foods, and Hydrolyzed Formulas." American Academy of Pediatrics. Accessed June 14, 2014. http://pediatrics.aappublications.org /content/121/1/183.long.

Healthychildren.org. "Discontinuing the Bottle." Accessed June 15, 2014. http:// www.healthychildren.org/English/ages -stages/baby/feeding-nutrition/Pages /Discontinuing-the-Bottle.aspx.

The Institute for Responsible Technology. "GMO Health Dangers." December 2013. Accessed June 14, 2014. http:// www.responsibletechnology.org/posts /gmo-health-dangers.

Mayo Clinic. "Infant Development: Milestones From 4 to 6." Accessed June 14, 2014. http://www.mayoclinic.org /healthy-living/infant-and-toddler -health/in-depth/infant-development /art-20048178.

National Institute of Environmental Health Sciences. "Bisphenol A (BPA)." Accessed June 14, 2014. http://www.niehs.nih.gov /health/topics/agents/sya-bpa.

National Institutes of Health Office of Dietary Supplements. "Vitamin A: Fact Sheet for Consumers." Accessed June 16, 2014. http://ods.od.nih.gov/factsheets /VitaminA-QuickFacts.

National Institutes of Health Office of Dietary Supplements. "Vitamin C: Fact Sheet for Consumers." Accessed June 16, 2014. http://ods.od.nih.gov/factsheets /VitaminC-QuickFacts.

National Institutes of Health Office of Dietary Supplements. "Vitamin E: Fact Sheet for Consumers." Accessed June 16, 2014. http://ods.od.nih.gov/factsheets /VitaminE-QuickFacts.

Organic Consumers Association. "Information on rBGH or rBST." Accessed June 13, 2014. https://www.organicconsumers.org/categories/rbgh.

Smith, Dr. Michelle Annette. "Homemade Baby Food—Make It Safely." FDA Office of Food Safety. Accessed June 14, 2014. http://www.foodsafety.gov/blog/homemade_babyfood.html.

United States Department of Agriculture. "Nutritional Needs of Infants." Accessed June 14, 2014. http://www.nal.usda.gov/wicworks/Topics/FG/Chapter1_NutritionalNeeds.pdf.

United States Department of Agriculture National Nutrient Database for Standard Reference. Release 25. U.S. Department of Agriculture, Agricultural Research Service. Accessed June 15, 2014. http://ndb.nal.usda.gov.

United States Department of Health and Human Services. "Dietary Guidelines for Americans, 2010." Accessed June 15, 2014. http://health.gov/dietaryguidelines/2010.asp.

United States Environmental Protection Agency. "Pesticides and Food: Why Children May Be Especially Sensitive to Pesticides." Accessed June 13, 2014. http://www.epa.gov/pesticides/food/pest.htm.

United States Food and Drug Administration. "FDA's Role in Regulating Safety of GE Foods." Accessed June 14, 2014. http://www.fda.gov/forconsumers/consumerupdates/ucm352067.htm.

United States Food and Drug Administration. Docket No. OlN-0458; "Food Labeling; Guidelines for Voluntary Nutrition Labeling of Raw Fruits, Vegetables, and Fish; Identification of the 20 Most Frequently Consumed Raw Fruits, Vegetables, and Fish"; 67FR. 12918, June 3, 2002. Accessed June 15, 2014. http://www.fda.gov/ohrms/dockets/dailys/02/jun02/060302/80047196.pdf.

United States Food and Drug Administration. "Report on the Food and Drug Administration's Review of the Safety of Recombinant Bovine Somatotropin." Accessed June 13, 2014. http://www.fda.gov/animalveterinary/safetyhealth/productsafetyinformation/ucm130321.htm.

University of Minnesota's Academic Health Center. "U of M Expert: Toddlers Can Go All In with Whole Milk." August 8, 2012. Accessed June 15, 2014. http://www.healthtalk.umn.edu/2012/08/08/u-of-m-expert-toddlers-can-go-all-in-with-whole-milk/.

World Action on Salt and Health. "How Does Salt Affect Children?" Accessed June 15, 2014. http://www.worldactiononsalt.com/salthealth/children.

World Health Organization. "Breastfeeding." Accessed June 16, 2014. http://www.who.int/topics/breastfeeding/en/.

Index

CPSIA information can be obtained
at www.ICGtesting.com
Printed in the USA
BVOW11s1032081116
467224BV00017B/90/P